Exam Secrets A2

Business Studies

David Floyd

Stephen Wood

Contents

Examination boards

AQA Assessment and Qualifications Alliance
Devas Street,
Manchester, M15 6EX
www.aqa.org.uk

EDEXCEL
Stewart House,
32 Russell Square,
London, WC1B 5DN
www.edexcel.org.uk

OCR Oxford Cambridge and RSA Examinations
1 Hills Road,
Cambridge, CB1 2EU
www.ocr.org.uk

CCEA Northern Ireland Council for Curriculum, Examinations and Assessment
29 Clarendon Road,
Belfast, BT1 3BG
www.ccea.org.uk

WJEC Welsh Joint Education Committee
245 Western Avenue,
Cardiff, CF5 2YX
www.wjec.co.uk

AQA

The three A2 Units are assessed by questions on a business decision-making case study (Unit 4), a report and essay of coursework (Unit 5), and questions based on a case study (Unit 6).

Edexcel

Assessment at A2 level is by compulsory questions (Unit 4), coursework or questions on a case study (Unit 5), and questions based on a synoptic pre-seen case study (Unit 6).

OCR

At A2 level, each optional Unit is tested based on an unseen case study, and there is a coursework project or thematic enquiry, and a Business Strategy paper based on a pre-issued case study.

CCEA

At A2 level, there is an external examination for Unit 4, either coursework or an exam based on an unseen case study, and questions based on a pre-seen case study.

WJEC

At A2 level, Unit 4 is assessed by two part-structured questions, Unit 5 by either coursework or an investigative study, and Unit 6 by questions based on a case study.

A2 exams

Different types of questions

Structured questions

In A level Business Studies exams, unit tests often use structured questions requiring both short answers and more extended answers. These questions are often in several parts, each of which may be further subdivided. They may be linked directly to data on a given context in the form of a paragraph or short article about a real or imagined business situation. This introductory data provides the major part of the information to be used, and indicates clearly what the question is about.

Structured questions are popular at A2 level. The parts to these questions become progressively more demanding as you work your way through them.

Extended answers

Business Studies questions requiring more extended answers may form part of structured questions, or may form separate questions. These may also be linked to a 'scenario' or case study, and are often used to assess your ability to communicate ideas and to assemble a logical argument. The synoptic assessment units will require some extended answers that test your ability to integrate your understanding of various Business Studies content and themes.

The 'correct' answers to extended questions are often less well-defined than those requiring shorter answers. Examiners have a list of points for which credit is awarded up to the maximum for the question.

What examiners look for

- Examiners are obviously looking for correct points, although these may not match the wording in the examiner's marking scheme exactly.

- Your answer will score high marks if it contains accurate content and shows that you can apply, analyse and evaluate this content in the context of the question. You will not receive extra marks for writing a lot of words or through simply repeating information.

- Examiners expect you to reach a logical conclusion based on the arguments presented in your answer.

What makes an A, C and E grade candidate?

Obviously, you want to get the highest grade you possibly can. The way to do this is to make sure you have a good all-round knowledge and understanding of Business Studies.

- **A grade candidates** have a wide knowledge of Business Studies and can apply that knowledge to new situations. They are equally strong in all of the modules. A likely minimum mark for an A grade candidate is 75%.

- **C grade candidates** have a reasonable knowledge of Business Studies, but they are less effective when applying their knowledge to new situations. They may also have weaknesses in some of the modules. A likely minimum mark for a C grade candidate is 50%.

- **E grade candidates** have a limited knowledge of Business Studies, and have not learnt how to apply their ideas effectively to new situations. They find it harder to express their knowledge, and fail to give full answers. A likely minimum mark for an E grade is 40%.

Successful revision

Revision skills

- Develop a 'revision routine', e.g. by doing revision in the same place and about the same time each day.

- Prepare a revision plan for a topic, e.g. review next day, then re-read two weeks later.

- Start with a topic with which you are familiar.

- Re-read topics, to reinforce your learning.

- If you make revision notes, identify key points such as the main business theme or issue.

- Vary the style of your notes, e.g. by producing 'spider diagrams', patterned notes or mnemonics.

- Limit the time you spend (e.g. 30 to 40 minutes) before taking a break.

- Stop before you get too tired.

- Leave something easy with which to start your revision the next day.

- Don't stay up late the night before an exam trying to learn new topics. You will have forgotten much of it by the morning, and the lack of sleep may affect your performance in the exam.

Practice questions

This book is designed to help you get better results.

- Study the grade A and C candidates' answers, and see if you could have done better.

- Try the exam practice questions, and then check the answers.

- Make sure you understand why the answers given are correct.

- When you feel ready, try the A2 mock exam papers.

If you perform well on the questions in this book, you should do well in the examination.

Planning and timing your answers in the exam

- You should spend the first few minutes of the assessment reading through the whole question paper.

- When answering structured questions, do not feel that you have to complete one part before starting the next. The further you are into a question, the more difficult the marks can be to obtain. If you run out of ideas, go on to the next part/question.

- You need to respond to as many parts of questions as possible. You will not score well if you spend so long trying to perfect the first questions that you do not reach later questions at all.

- Use the mark allocation to guide you on how much to write, and on how many different points to make.

- Plan your answers: don't write down the first thing that comes into your head.

- Make sure your plan reminds you to refer to any relevant information in the given case study/situation.

- Make sure you give a balanced answer where required.

- Allow some time at the end to read through your answers.

How to boost your grade

Organisation

- Organise your main and revision notes carefully, keeping them in a file.
- If you use highlighter pens or underlining to emphasise sections of your notes, make sure you limit their use to the really important points.

Research

- Spend some time reading the 'broadsheet' newspapers or other sources of up-to-date business information.
- Make brief summaries of business developments: you may be able to mention these developments when answering the exam questions.
- This research will also help you with coursework projects.

Answering the question

- Make sure you read and study the data before you tackle the questions.
- You'll rarely find that a question is one-sided in outcome, so always give a balanced answer/conclusion.
- Keep referring back to the question for information you may need to extract or comment on in your answer.
- If you decide to start by answering the question you think you can do best first, don't spend over-long on this question because you will lose valuable time needed to construct answers to the other questions.

Words and figures

- Marks are not only given for correct spelling, punctuation and grammar: you'll score higher marks if you can use business terms and language suitably.
- Study and become familiar with the key terms used in the main functional areas: marketing, accounting, human resource management and production.
- Be particularly careful when using accounting terms: for example, profit and cash are different, and so are profit and profitability.
- You should make sure that your answer is clear, easy to read and concise.
- If possible, estimate any numerical answer first.
- Check any calculations you have made, and make sure that your answer is sensible. Is it given in the correct units (e.g. £000)? Does it look right? Show all your working.

Diagrams and formulae

- Check whether you will be given formulae in the exam, e.g. for standard deviation or time series calculations. If so, you don't need to waste time memorising them, BUT you still need to understand how the formula is constructed, why it exists and what it calculates.
- You should make sure that any graphs, charts or other diagrams are correctly labelled, given a relevant heading, and have a suitable scale that fills (most of) the graph paper.

Chapter 1

External environment and influences

Questions with model answers

Charities

Examiner's Commentary

WHEN BIG BUSINESS PLAYS ITS PART, GIVING MONEY ISN'T THE ONLY WAY TO HELP by Ellen Davies

Are donations simply made for selfish reasons, to buy reputation? Some companies deny that their motives are anything but altruistic – but, says Peter Hunt, community programme manager for Shell UK, giving money to good causes for purely philanthropic reasons is unethical: 'The money belongs to our shareholders and we have to make it grow. I have a moral problem with giving money away without any benefit to the business.' Shell's total contribution to charity in the UK last year was about £5.5 million, and only £1.8 million of that was cash.

'Giving money is often the least effective way of helping,' Hunt argues. 'It's like pouring water into the desert.'

Shell prefers to work with charities to build long-term programmes, looking at areas where there are business links – education, enterprise and the environment: 'We look for the people who are doing good work and pushing things forward, where we can contribute something significant.'

Source: adapted from the *Daily Telegraph*, 14 December, 1995

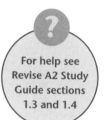

For help see Revise A2 Study Guide sections 1.3 and 1.4

ANITA AND GORDON RODDICK LAUNCHING AN ADVERTISEMENT

Anita and Gordon Roddick are breaking with one of Body Shop's longest-held traditions by launching an advertisement on Monday. The advert, though, will not be promoting Body Shop, but a Channel 4 documentary due to be screened that evening, called *The Drilling Fields*.

It concerns Shell's exploration activities in Nigeria and the opposition to them from the Ogoni tribe, whose tribal lands are affected. Roddick and the programme makers claim 1000 people have died in clashes between the Ogoni and government forces protecting Shell representatives.

Source: the *Daily Telegraph*, 21 May, 1994

(a) Analyse the possible effects for Body Shop of their concern for ethical issues. [8]

(b) With reference to *both* articles, evaluate whether businesses are becoming more ethically and socially responsible. [12]

External environment and influences

Examiner's Commentary

(a) Body Shop will be able to sell more of its products because at the moment it is very popular to be ethically and environmentally friendly. People who dislike Shell's treatment of the Ogoni tribe will feel more positive towards Body Shop and so buy more of its products. Body Shop will gain good publicity from this venture and this explains why it does not have to spend as much on advertising and marketing as other competitors. It is able to rely far more on the brand loyalty of its customers. The people who are not bothered about Shell's treatment of the Ogoni will probably not be likely to buy from Body Shop in any case.

> This is an interesting point, but it is a shame it has not been explained.

Another effect of Body Shop being interested in ethical matters is that it will be able to attract better-quality and more committed employees. People will like working for Body Shop and will be less likely to leave.

> Although it does not state so explicitly in the question, if you are asked for the effects of something happening you should always look to provide a balanced argument to gain more than half marks.

(b) In donating over £5 million to charity it is clear that Shell is trying to be more socially responsible. It knows that as a company it is seen as damaging to the environment, both because of petrol pollution and bad publicity surrounding the dumping of disused oil platforms at sea. It will be making these donations to help raise the public's opinion of it as a company.

However, it is likely that many potential customers of Shell will not be aware of its promotion of good causes and will not see it as being ethical.

The fact that their community programme manager clearly states that they are only making donations to charity where it makes business sense suggests that Shell is not being ethical at all and is rather doing it for the wrong reasons.

> It is a shame that this point was not developed.

Body Shop has always been a company with high ethical standards and its involvement with the publicity surrounding the Ogoni tribe does not provide any evidence that business is becoming more ethical.

> This answer suffers for two reasons. First, it does not really answer the question set. It generally explains the potential reasons for Shell's strategy for giving to charity, but does not analyse whether this means they are becoming more ethical. Second, it is primarily about Shell, and only mentions Body Shop as an afterthought. There should be a more balanced coverage of the two articles.

GRADE BOOSTER

> Many students come up with good ideas in their answers. Unfortunately, a lot of the time these ideas are not well explained.

Examiner's Commentary

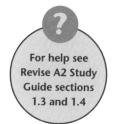

For help see
Revise A2 Study
Guide sections
1.3 and 1.4

(a) By showing a concern for ethical issues Body Shop may expect to maintain or improve their reputation and retain the customer's positive view of the company. Body Shop has relied on this brand loyalty from its customers in recent years as it has fought to compete against larger, more powerful competitors. It can be argued that it has been able to attract customers because of its ethical stance. Ethical concern may also attract better, more motivated staff, at a time when it is becoming increasingly difficult to recruit and retain good quality staff because of low unemployment. Recruiting staff who are sympathetic to Body Shop's ethical standpoint will mean that staff turnover, absenteeism, loyalty and ultimately productivity will be improved.

> This shows an awareness of current external factors.

However, it must also be recognised that ethical practices may act as a constraint. Body Shop's attitude towards animal testing at a time when this was common practice will have increased its costs. The time taken to research potential suppliers to ensure that they conform to Body Shop's ethical standards will have proven costly and ultimately may have denied it many suppliers. Even when a supplier is chosen, time and money will have to be spent to monitor continuously whether the supplier is keeping to the code of conduct required.

Body Shop may alienate many customers who are loyal to Shell, and believe that what they are doing in Nigeria is not wrong. The amount of time that Body Shop spend on promoting ethical issues of concern may mean that other aspects of managing the company are ignored or poorly carried out.

> The word 'analyse' in the question indicates that the pros and cons need to be covered with some discussion but certainly no attempt to evaluate is required.

(b) There is some evidence in the articles to support both sides of the argument about whether companies are becoming more ethical. Shell donated £5.5 million during 1995. This may indicate that they have a desire to see disadvantaged groups in society benefit. However, when one considers the size of this donation against the likely size of Shell's profits it may be seen as too little.

> Good to see that the writer of this answer does not take evidence solely at face value.

It is an interesting argument put forward by Peter Hunt. He is suggesting that actually making large contributions to charity is in itself unethical. This is of course seen from the point of view of shareholders, whose profits are their rewards from investing in Shell. Dividends are seen to be the payback for shareholders' risk taking. It may be argued that investing in such a large and financially successful company as Shell does not in fact possess much risk and dividends do not need to be so high. Peter Hunt is disregarding other stakeholders' views on this topic and suggests that Shell see their shareholders as being the most important stakeholder: not necessarily a very ethical approach to business.

External environment and influences

The comment about not 'giving money away without any benefit to the business' may indicate the true attitude to charitable donations by Shell. This statement suggests that they see it as a marketing exercise and they will only donate if the returns to Shell are greater than the cost. This may be regarded as an unethical attitude and indicative of most large companies' approach to donations. It would appear that Shell's contributions to charity come out of their marketing rather than their charitable donations budget.

Comparison of costs and benefits will usually be seen as evaluation.

In contrast to this, Body Shop has taken time and effort to promote a campaign about an issue directly unrelated to its line of business. Any campaign against Shell cannot be regarded as being part of marketing, as Shell and Body Shop have completely unrelated lines of business. Body Shop has spent its own money on producing the advertisement which is not promoting its product, although the cynical attitude may be that it is still good promotion.

A good answer will always identify opposite points of view.

In conclusion, it is very difficult to conclude whether companies are becoming more ethical or not. The information provided in the two articles is very limited and there is no way to allow a comparison with previous years. Also, the information gives a mixed picture about the behaviour of business. On the one hand, Body Shop has always maintained a very high profile concerning matters of ethical and socially responsible behaviour. On the other hand, Shell and the oil industry in general, have had to react to considerable bad publicity about the safety of oil platforms, the dumping of these in the North Sea and the long-term costs of pollution from fossil fuels.

Another acceptable way to evaluate. The lack of suitable evidence to make a balanced judgement.

External environment and influences

Exam practice questions

A TIGHTENING LABOUR MARKET

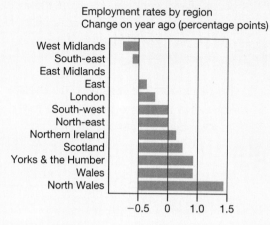

Employment rates by region
Change on year ago (percentage points)

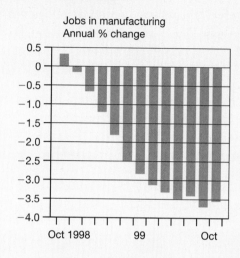

Jobs in manufacturing
Annual % change

Sources: ONS; Primark Datastream

Growing bonuses are helping to push up pay increases, fuelling expectations that the Bank of England may soon need to raise interest rates again. October alone saw average earnings growth speed up to 5.1% compared to 4.6% in September. Much of the increase is due to increased bonus payments in real estate, business services, the retail sector and the banking and financial services sectors.

The Bank may also be concerned at signs of tightening in the labour market, with another fall in unemployment. The number of people in work rose by an estimated 66 000 between August and October and this means that nearly 27.5 million people are in paid employment. Andrew Oswald, Professor of Economics at Warwick University, warns that inflation may soon be a problem and that, 'a tightening labour market and rising oil prices could spell trouble for the economy by the middle of next year'.

Source: Adapted from *The Financial Times,* 16 December, 1999

(a) Briefly explain the meaning of the following:

   (i) inflation

   (ii) a tightening labour market. [4]

(b) Explain why rising average earnings may or may not contribute to inflationary pressure in the United Kingdom economy. [6]

(c) Discuss the arguments for and against the raising of interest rates, by the Bank of England, as a means of solving the inflationary problems indicated in the passage. [8]

[WJEC June 2000]

External environment and influences

②

PAPER TIGER

'You must have found this quite a change' was a comment Mark Peters had heard a lot recently. Mark had spent many years working for a relatively small, old people's charity. While there he had developed a reputation as an innovative, forward-thinking manager who was credited with much of the success of the charity. Three months ago he had been appointed Chief Executive of New Paper Ltd, a manufacturer of paper and board products, set up by his father over thirty-five years ago.   5

Mark felt at home the moment he went back to the business. He had worked there during holidays from school and university. In many ways it seemed inevitable that Mark would eventually run the firm, just as he fully intended his own daughter to follow him as Chief Executive one day.   10

A real challenge for Mark was coming to terms with the different scale of his new position. At the charity, Mark had adopted a direct, hands-on approach, giving him a clear insight into all areas of the charity's operations. He had already found it impossible to be as involved in the day-to-day running of New Paper Ltd, and often found that visiting the firm's processing plant carried a high opportunity cost in that   15
work piled up for him back in the office.

Mark was realistic enough to see that manufacturing in the UK had been having a difficult time in recent years. High exchange rates and stiff competition from foreign firms with lower costs were generally being blamed for the downturn in the sector. There was little sign that government economic policy was likely to change   20
dramatically in the near future to provide aid for industry, although some people in the firm believed these problems might be eased by the UK joining the single European currency within the next two years.

There was, though, a dark cloud on the horizon for New Paper Ltd. Mark's father had spent a lot of time and money gaining a foothold in the USA market. There were   25
strong rumours circulating that the USA was about to introduce trade barriers to protect its home industry from foreign competition. As well as the direct loss of trade, it also threw into doubt the firm's policy of expanding in this, the world's largest market (see Appendix A).

Mark, though, was keen to continue the process of giving the firm a world-wide   30
profile. He had already been talking to the rest of the board about starting operations in a new market elsewhere in the world. In particular, he was looking at Asia. Traditionally there had been a low level of demand there, but Mark felt there was tremendous scope for development in this market. An estimated initial investment of around £5m was likely to be needed to set up this part of the business.   35

A particular frustration had been the inability of the firm to originate new ideas. As Firoza, the product manager, had said, 'There is little scope for developing much in the way of product differentiation in this market. To the end user, one sheet of paper is pretty much like another, unless you go for very cheap, which no one wants to use, or the very expensive, which few people feel is worthwhile. We need to find other   40
ways of competing.'

One change that Mark was determined to bring in, was in the firm's stance on environmental issues. Perhaps because of his background of working in a charity, Mark placed a high value on taking the right moral stance on business issues. At an early board meeting he had deliberately raised the question of the firm's ethical position. He had expected a tough time, defending his position against other members of the family, who seemed to have more of an emphasis on profits.

To his surprise, and pleasure, the meeting had ended with broad agreement on the firm publicly stating its moral position. A working party had also been set up to rewrite the firm's mission statement to reflect its ethics, as well as setting quality standards for what was to become an annual environmental audit of the firm.

His pleasure was reduced, though, when he later overheard one of his colleagues saying 'This new ethical policy sounds great. If we use it right, it should bring us lots of new customers. It's a valuable marketing tool'.

Having been in his new job for three months, Mark felt that he was sufficiently established to allow him to weigh-up the current situation facing New Paper Ltd.

On the one hand, New Paper Ltd, along with most manufacturing firms, was in a difficult trading position. At home in the UK, the total market in paper goods was around 13 million tonnes, but UK production was only 6 million tonnes. The massive in-roads being made by foreign producers have been helped recently by world economic conditions. In addition, although economic activity is forecast to improve in the next few years, the main markets for paper, such as advertising and graphics, remain weak.

On the other hand, Mark was optimistic that there was scope for New Paper Ltd to develop new markets. Although the firm had enjoyed some success in the United States, Mark felt that there was likely to be a massive increase in the amount of paper consumed in Asia in the near future. Longer term, he also had hopes for an enlarged European Union creating an increased demand for paper products in Eastern Europe.

Overall, Mark was convinced the future for New Paper Ltd lay in a strategy of market development. Despite, or perhaps because of, the increasing use of computers, it seemed likely the demand for paper would increase in the future. Mark felt his job was to make sure New Paper Ltd was in the right position to benefit from this increase.

Source: adapted from www.ppic.org.uk

APPENDIX A

Per Capita Consumption of Paper and Board (kgs) (Selected nations)			
Country	**1990**	**2000**	**2010 (estimated)**
USA	311	332	385
Germany	232	233	220
UK	169	216	230
Asia	20	28	45
Eastern Europe	35	29	30

APPENDIX B

Extract from the Accounts of New Paper Ltd (year ended 31 December 2002)		
	2002 £m	**2001 £m**
Total Sales	7.5	7.8
UK Sales	6.2	5.9
USA Sales	1.3	1.9
Operating Profit	1.0	1.3
Net Profit	0.6	0.8
Return on Capital	4.1%	5.5%
Gearing	37%	37%
Acid Test	1.2	1.4

(a) British manufacturing firms have faced serious problems in recent years, partly due to government economic policy. Discuss the ways a firm such as New Paper Ltd could attempt to influence such economic policy decisions. [14]

(b) Discuss the possible impact on New Paper Ltd of the UK joining the single European currency. [16]

(c) Evaluate the view that an ethical stance is 'a valuable marketing tool' (lines 53–54). [16]

[AQA January 2003]

Answers

(1) (a) (i) *Knowledge/Understanding*

A sustained increase in the average price of products in an economy over a period of time. **(1–2 marks)**

(ii) *Knowledge/Understanding*

When unemployment is falling and it is therefore more difficult to recruit employees. It usually leads to wages being forced up because of excess demand for labour. **(1–2 marks)**

(b) *Knowledge*

Rising wages lead to demand-pull inflation as well as cost-push inflation.

(1–2 marks)

Understanding/Application

- If earnings go up then workers have more money to spend, leading to increased demand and higher prices.

- Higher wages are a rise in costs to a business, and if not matched by an increase in productivity, will lead to price rises.

- Both of these may not lead to inflation as some or all of the extra wages may be saved or taken in taxes. Also, firms making reasonable profits may be able to absorb an increase in labour costs by reducing profits. **(3–6 marks)**

(c) *Knowledge/Understanding*

- Higher interest rates make it harder and more expensive to borrow money and more attractive to save money. This will reduce demand so reducing the pressure on inflation.

- Exchange rates are likely to rise because of higher interest rates so leading to cheaper imported raw materials, which reduce cost pressures on UK firms.

(1–3 marks)

Analysis

- The high level of imports into the UK means that higher exchange rates due to higher interest rates have a particularly strong effect on the UK economy.

- It is difficult to predict the exact size and timing of the impact of higher interest rates and so they are not reliable at controlling inflation.

- The consequences of high unemployment caused by falls in spending and demand, as well as a fall in exports caused by the strong pound, are particularly unattractive side effects. **(4–6 marks)**

Evaluation

The suitability of using interest rates to control inflation can be questioned because of the mentioned drawbacks and the time lag between interest rate change and effect on inflation. Nowadays there is less of a link between higher interest rates and reduced post-mortgage income because of the increased availability and popularity of fixed interest rate deals. **(7–8 marks)**

| examiner's tip | To gain top marks you need to be able to recognise the wider implications of a rise in interest rates. You may also briefly refer to other means of solving inflationary pressure, including supply-side policies and fiscal policy. |

External environment and influences

(2) (a) *Knowledge/Application*

Methods that New Paper Ltd could use to influence economic policy include:

- Lobbying parliament directly via their local MP.
- As a larger group such as an industry association, e.g. The Paper Federation of Great Britain, or the CBI.
- Indirectly, government's attention may be gained by the firm making threats about job losses, plant closures or moving production abroad.   **(1–5 marks)**

Analysis

- Given Mark's previous experience working for a charity he may have greater knowledge of the political processes and gaining favour with the government. However, any government has many different economic aims and the UK government would appear to have decided that protecting manufacturing is not a priority, thus making it less responsive.
- Although we do not know the size of the workforce at New Paper Ltd, we can infer from comments about the size of the business and the inability for Mark to be involved in the day-to-day running of the business that there are a lot of employees. It may therefore be possible that any threat to the future retention of these workers will attract some attention. The government will not want to see substantial redundancies, with the associated financial cost of state benefits, the impact on the local economy and suppliers and any effect on social factors, e.g. crime rate and poverty.   **(6–8 marks)**

Evaluation

- Ultimately, it could be argued that there is little wisdom in spending time and money on what is likely to be a fruitless attempt to influence the government. The firm has much more pressing needs, such as potential USA trade barriers and possible entry into the Asian market.
- There may be more success in New Paper Ltd taking advantage of the encouragement being given both by UK and EU governments to 'environmentally-friendly' business practice. Any improvement in the firm's ethical stance on such issues as recycling or production of paper from renewable sources, may be more likely to curry favour with government authorities.   **(9–14 marks)**

(b) *Knowledge*

Theoretical benefits of the UK joining the Euro are that costs of changing currency are removed, prices are more transparent and one large common currency market is created. On the other hand, interest rates will be set by the European Central Bank, for the benefit of the whole of Europe.   **(1–3 marks)**

Understanding/Application

- The fact that there will be a common currency means that if New Paper Ltd sell their products in Europe they will not have to worry about the difficulties caused by setting prices in a foreign currency. With separate currencies, if the exchange rate appreciates or depreciates between agreeing a price and payment being made New Paper Ltd may gain or lose out in terms of the sterling price.

- By having a common currency it will make it harder for New Paper Ltd to hide any inefficiencies that lead to relatively higher prices, compared to their European competitors. European buyers will find it easier to identify the cheapest producers of the product. **(4–6 marks)**

Analysis

- Although the costs of transactions with other EU countries will be reduced, there is no evidence that New Paper Ltd sell any of their goods to the EU. We are told that their main market is the USA and the UK. There is a mention of the company looking to expand possibly into Asia or Eastern Europe, but not the European countries currently covered by the common currency.

- The financial management strategies adopted by the European Central Bank (ECB) may not be advantageous to UK firms such as New Paper Ltd. The early part of this century has seen the UK economy in a boom phase of the trade cycle against the recessions seen in many European countries. The necessary low interest rates set by the ECB would have created excessive demand in the UK economy, that may have led to price and wage inflation that would have made New Look Paper Ltd even more uncompetitive against European Competitors. **(7–10 marks)**

Evaluation

- Entry by the UK into the Euro may in fact only benefit the European producers of paper and board products. The removal of transaction costs will make it considerably cheaper for them to sell into the UK and, with lower costs in many European countries, it will be likely that they can undercut New Paper Ltd.

- For a company that is based in the UK, looking to trade with the USA and Asia, the benefits listed of increasing ease of access to European markets may be outweighed by the drawbacks mentioned. Ultimately, the overall effect will depend on the degree of competitive advantage that New Paper Ltd has over European competitors as well as the influence that joining the Euro may have on the management of New Paper Ltd, in terms of changing their strategy towards European sales. **(11–16 marks)**

External environment and influences

(c) *Knowledge*

- An ethical stance can lead to a unique selling point, positive publicity and the ability to charge higher prices. **(1–3 marks)**

Understanding/Application

- The fact that any products produced by New Paper Ltd. can state that, for example, they are 'made from sustainable forests' will lead to many consumers who are now conscious about using 'green products' choosing them over other competitors.
- Because the product has a USP, consumers may be more willing to pay a higher price without it affecting the volume sold. **(4–6 marks)**

Analysis

- It could also be argued that an ethical stance will affect profits. For New Paper Ltd to follow an ethical policy it will undoubtedly cost more money. For example, purchasing wood pulp from sustainable forests will be more expensive than purchasing from companies that do not replant trees. This will make New Paper's products more expensive and in what we are told is a competitive market – 'massive in-roads being made by foreign producers' (line 60) – this additional cost will seriously affect profit.
- New Paper Ltd may be able to benefit from their ethical stance not just in marketing to the customer but also to potential employees. New Paper Ltd may gain a reputation as an ethical employer, in terms of fair pay, respect for worker rights and flexible working for parents with young children. This will give them a greater choice of the best employees available in the labour market. **(7–10 marks)**

Evaluation

- Another complication is that much of New Paper Ltd's products will not be sold to the end consumer, but to businesses such as greetings cards firms or packaging companies. These companies will be also looking to keep their costs down. The consumer on the 'high street' will ultimately make purchasing decisions based on the ethical stance of these companies, rather than a company making up part of the supply chain such as New Paper Ltd.
- In the end, the success of an ethical stance will be determined by the demand for this sort of business approach in their core markets. For example, the USA has a good ethical record whereas in Asia it is much less of an issue. Also, the degree of ethical standards throughout the industry will affect the level of competitive advantage that New Paper Ltd would gain from adopting a clear ethical policy. **(11–16 marks)**

Chapter 2

Business organisations, structure and growth

Questions with model answers

Whitbread sells all 3000 pubs

Examiner's Commentary

Whitbread heralded the end of an era yesterday when the former brewing giant put its 3000-strong pub estate up for sale to concentrate on leisure activities.

The sale of the pub estate, which is estimated to be worth £1.5 billion, comes hard on the heels of the £400m disposal of Whitbread's brewing activities to Interbrew.

The sale will leave Whitbread to concentrate on its hotel brands Marriott and Travel Inn, restaurant brands Beefeater, Bella Pasta and Café Rouge and the David Lloyd leisure business.

'We are selling a business that is outperforming its marketplace with a management with a high reputation', Sir John Banham, the chairman, said yesterday. 'This is just a continuation of our strategy to reduce dependence on beer.' He said that two-thirds of the money derived from the sale of the pub estate would be distributed among shareholders. This would amount to around £2 a share. Whitbread shares shot up $37\frac{1}{2}$ p to 469p at the news.

Sir John said the company was working to improve lacklustre brands such as Beefeater, by rebranding most of its 258 restaurants, with about 80 becoming a new concept, Out and Out, aimed at middle-class diners. The whole group had to achieve like-for-like sales growth of 5%, which would produce 'double digit profits growth'. Over the last half year, hotels' underlying sales rose by 9.8%, with operating profits up 85% to £46m. Restaurants' comparable sales were up 2.2% with operating profits up 8.2% to £65.7m. Fitness club profits rose 26% to £13.1m.

Source: adapted from the *Daily Telegraph*, 20 October & 1 November, 2000

?

For help see Revise A2 Study Guide sections 2.1 and 2.3

(a) Discuss the possible reasons why Whitbread decided to sell off its brewing activities to Interbrew. [10]

(b) Evaluate how the strategy of rebranding the Beefeater restaurants will affect Whitbread's stakeholders. [12]

C grade candidate – mark scored 11/22

(a) Whitbread may have sold their brewing activities for a number of reasons. They may have needed the money gained from selling this part of the business. £400 million is a lot of money and it may have allowed them to do other things. We are told in the passage that the hotel part of the company has grown by 9.8%. This fast-growing sector is also producing very high profits. If more money is invested in these two sectors Whitbread may benefit to a greater extent than they currently do in the brewing industry.

Brewing may have been uncompetitive and unprofitable. Selling the brewery will mean that another specialist firm such as Interbrew can try to make the business more efficient and eventually profitable. It may be the case that Whitbread have diversified too much and this has meant that they are unable to spend enough time building up the brewing side of the business. Alternatively, they may find that their managers are now more geared up to other sectors of the leisure industry, especially as they have now announced that they are to sell their pub estate, and do not have the knowledge and skill to turn the brewery around financially.

> This answer, although only dealing with a couple of possible reasons, does try to explain the reasoning. It gains more than half marks because it uses some evidence from the article to analyse what may have happened.

(b) Stakeholders are those individuals or groups with a direct interest in a company's actions. I am going to examine the effect on employees, banks, customers and the community.

The employees may be affected because the new restaurant will employ better quality workers. This will mean that the present staff are made redundant.

> Are these two restaurants going to be so different that some or all of the staff cannot be retrained?

The banks may be concerned because the rebranding will cost money that Whitbread may have to borrow. Also, if the new restaurants are not successful, this may affect the company's ability to repay interest on other loans they may have.

Customers will benefit because they will get a new type of restaurant. They will have more choice, although the prices will be higher.

> What about the fact that the new brand is really being aimed at a different market segment?

The local community may suffer because some workers will now be out of work, although some others will have gained jobs.

GRADE BOOSTER   Greater breadth and depth of argument are needed at A2 level.

A grade candidate – mark scored 21/22

Examiner's Commentary

(a) It may appear surprising that Whitbread has decided to sell off its brewing activities when we are told that the business is 'outperforming its marketplace with a management with a high reputation'. If this sector of the business is doing so well then we must assume that Whitbread has good reason to sell up. First, although we are told that it is performing well and has good management, we are not told whether the brewing sector is profitable. In recent years this industry has seen a lot of competition with many large brewers merging. It may well be that the brewing industry is not particularly profitable and, although Whitbread are doing well, this is still not as good as in the other sectors of their business.

Second, if Whitbread had a long-term strategy of selling their pubs, which they have now announced, the sale of the brewing sector may have been decided as a logical part of this overall strategy. Without pubs to sell their beer, it may have been considered too difficult and expensive to find suitable distribution channels.

Good incorporation of issues learnt in the AS part of the course.

Third, we are told that the sale of the brewing sector has raised £400 million. This is a sizeable amount of finance to allow the expansion into other more profitable sectors of the leisure industry. The large and growing revenue and profit figures quoted for these sectors will make further investment in them very attractive. There is a danger that if Whitbread do not carry out the necessary investment now they will be left behind. This level of investment may not be possible with more traditional sources of finance, such as borrowing. (Whitbread may in fact be unable to raise any more finance via banks or shareholders.)

It is good to see an answer that does not assume facts that are unknown, but raises the issues that may apply.

Finally, the decision to 'reduce dependence on beer' suggests that Whitbread recognise that they should not rely on this sector in the future. In today's market it is dangerous to rely on one particular product, especially if that product is not highly profitable.

In conclusion, it is clear that Whitbread have sold their brewing interests as part of a clear long-term strategy. It has raised finance for expansion in more profitable markets and has allowed them to have a more diverse portfolio of products. It may well be that Whitbread saw Interbrew as a company who could take over their brewing activities and because of their specialisation be more efficient at it, so making greater profits. In this case, Whitbread may have been able to receive a price for the brewing assets greater than their value on the Whitbread balance sheet.

This is a good conclusion. It does not just repeat points made earlier. There is a good attempt to put together the main issues.

For help see Revise A2 Study Guide sections 2.1 and 2.3

Business organisations, structure and growth

21

A grade continued

(b) When considering the impact on different stakeholders the main issue is that each of them has different objectives. Whitbread must balance these objectives to ensure that all stakeholders are happy and that conflict is minimised.

One of the main groups of stakeholders are Whitbread's shareholders. They will expect a good return from their investment in the form of dividends and an increase in the share price. By rebranding some of the Beefeater restaurants Whitbread are aiming to increase their appeal, especially amongst middle-class diners. These diners will have more disposable income and so will expect a different quality of service than that currently offered. This may mean that prices can be higher, although this will not automatically mean more profit, as costs will presumably also be higher.

In fact, the extra costs in the short run of carrying out a rebranding strategy may mean that any benefits will be in the long run. Therefore, shareholders may see a fall in their dividend and share price initially. Growth in the restaurant sector appears slow at the moment compared to the other sectors in which Whitbread are involved. From the shareholders' viewpoint they might have preferred to see current marketing efforts in the faster growing hotel or fitness club sectors.

The customer is another important stakeholder. The switch in target market will mean that some customers will find that their local Beefeater restaurant will now be rebranded and possibly be outside their price-bracket. These customers will feel neglected and may desert other Whitbread-owned companies. The new 'Out and Out' restaurants will be targeted at new customers who may become vital assets to all of Whitbread's companies. Whitbread may feel that the new restaurant brand will better attract the type of customer currently loyal to Whitbread in their fitness clubs and hotels.

Suppliers will also be affected as some raw materials and components used in the new restaurants will be different from before. Better quality food, a higher standard of furniture and different advertising channels may mean that some suppliers are replaced.

The employees may also be greatly affected. To provide a higher level of service the chefs and waiting-on staff may need to be retrained. This may however be viewed as an advantage for them, as it will increase their skills and qualifications, as well as making them more employable in the future. They may also see their wages being increased.

It is clear to see that all stakeholders will be affected by the proposed change in different ways. Ultimately, the magnitude of the effect will vary, depending on how successful this rebranding exercise is. If it is successful and increases profits in the long run, shareholders, customers and employees will clearly benefit. It may also mean that more of the Beefeater restaurants are rebranded. If, however, the strategy is a failure, employees may lose their jobs, shareholders will see smaller dividends and customers will regard Whitbread as a failure.

This is an excellent start, which immediately highlights the potential conflict of objectives.

Any attempt to assess long-run versus short-run issues will be rewarded highly.

The topic of stakeholders is one that occurs throughout the course. Notice how when it is dealt with in the A2 part of the course it is much more integrated with other issues, such as Marketing and Human Resources.

1

OLIGOPOLY – BAD NEWS FOR HOLIDAYMAKERS?

The outlook for the small holiday firms and holidaymakers is looking as gloomy as an English summer at the moment.

The first problem is whether the results of recent mergers and takeovers are going to lead to higher prices and less choice for consumers. More than two-thirds of overseas holidays are in the hands of Thomson, Airtours, Thomas Cook and First Choice. The recent merger of Thomas Cook and Carlson now means this group owns one in five of all travel agencies, operating nearly 1400 agencies in the UK.
Of 21 million holidays on sale in June 1998 the 'big four' accounted for 14.2 million. The small independent agents, such as the 156 members of the Association of Independent Tour Operators (AITO), expect to sell only 2 million holidays between them, about half that of the Thomson group. The independents fear they will be squeezed out of hotels and airlines by the superior buying power of their dominant rivals and that competition and consumer choice will suffer. It is not only in the ownership of agencies and holidays that the small firms feel threatened. Charter airlines such as Britannia Airways, Air 2000, Airtours International and Caledonian are also in the hands of the 'big four'. AITO has now written to the Office of Fair Trading urging government action to prevent further concentration of ownership.

At the same time the industry is having to cope with the effects of increasing fuel taxes, departure tax, changes in interest rates and fluctuations in exchange rates set against a background of statistics that suggest the economy is going into recession.

Source: Adapted from *The Times Weekend*, Saturday 10 October, 1998
by Tom Chesshyre and Jannette Hyde

(a) Explain why the 'big four' may seek to avoid reducing prices to customers. [2]

(b) Evaluate mergers and takeovers as a strategy for growth. [8]

(c) How would you account for the continued survival and success of so many small agents in the holiday industry? [6]

[Edexcel June 2000]

Business organisations, structure and growth

MULTINATIONALS – GOOD OR BAD?

UK consumers have a choice of over 5000 chocolate lines available from 150 000 different outlets. On average a UK citizen spends £1.80 on chocolate every week. Three producers dominate the chocolate market in the UK. Cadbury have a 28% market share, with both Mars and Nestlé having about 24% of the market. Although chocolate manufacturing provides steady employment and job security for tens of thousands of UK employees in locations such as York, Birmingham and Slough, the industry also generates jobs throughout the world.

Chocolate cannot be made without the vital ingredient – the cocoa bean. Cocoa is grown in Central and South America, the west coast of Africa and more recently South East Asia. Eight countries – Ivory Coast, Ghana, Indonesia, Nigeria, Brazil, Cameroon, Ecuador and Malaysia supply 88% of world output. Over 40% of the world's supply comes from the Ivory Coast, where cocoa is grown mainly on over 600 000 small, family-owned farms.

As a major buyer, Nestlé seeks to be as closely involved in the supply chain as possible, to ensure quality and fairness. Nestlé participates in a process to examine potential problems of forced child labour on cocoa farms in West Africa. This is being done on an industry-wide basis, in consultation with governments, labour organisations and Non-Governmental Organisations (NGO).

Source: Nestlé – *The Times 100* (8th edition)

Answers on pages 26–28 **Answers** on pages 26–28 **Answers** on pages 26–28

Nestlé is the world's largest food company, controlling about half of the global baby food market, setting marketing trends, which influence other companies. This Swiss multinational produces baby milk powder for retail in developing countries. According to UNICEF, one and a half million children die every year from unsafe bottle feeding in developing countries. The high status Western products hold in third world countries, together with the lack of education, has led to the preference of Nestle's powdered milk over capable mothers' breastfeeding.

Nestlé abuse their power in third world countries. One of Nestlé's most successful marketing tactics is to give free or subsidised baby milk powder to hospitals. In many cases, enough milk is given to ensure that most, if not all of the hospital's newborn babies are bottle fed. Mothers are often given a sample tin to take home. Giving bottles to newborns makes breastfeeding failure more likely. The baby is then dependent on artificial baby milk. Once home, the mother has to buy the milk for herself. Bottle feeding is very expensive and so poor mothers often over-dilute the powder to make it last longer. This leads to malnutrition. In poor conditions, the water mixed with the milk is often unsafe, leading to diarrhoea, dehydration and often death.

Nestlé baby milk powder labels are printed in inappropriate languages. Instructions and health warnings on packaging are often either absent, not prominently displayed or in an inappropriate language. All of these actions directly contravene the Code regulating the marketing of baby milk. When questioned about inadequate labelling in South Africa, Nestlé stated that, 'due to the cost restraints of small runs it has not been viable to change languages for specific export countries.'

Source: adapted from www.mcspotlight.org and www.umu.man.ac.uk

(a) To what extent is Nestlé's success due to its size? [12]

(b) Evaluate the impact of multinationals, such as Nestlé, on a host country. [12]

Answers

(1) (a) *Knowledge/Understanding*

Because the firms are interdependent and oligopoly-like in structure they need to avoid a price war. Price stability is important for everyone's survival.

(1–2 marks)

(b) *Knowledge*

A merger is where two, or more, companies choose to combine and become one. A takeover is where one, usually dominant firm, acquires another firm.

(1–2 marks)

Understanding/Application

Growth via merger or takeover allows:

- A quicker way to increase sales turnover
- Entry into ready made markets that allow access to different types of holidaymakers
- A reduction in competition that will allow tour operators to be more efficient.

(3–4 marks)

Analysis

- The acquisition of another business may well lead to quicker growth but may lead to problems internally in the company. The bringing together of two groups of staff from different organisational cultures may lead to communication and management issues, ultimately leading to lower than expected gains in efficiency.
- If a company does not do sufficient research it may find that the company being taken over or merged with is inefficient or unsuitable.
- There is a danger that over-expansion may lead to financial problems, such as gearing as well as attracting the attention of the Competition Commission.

(5–6 marks)

Evaluation

Ultimately, the success of a merger or takeover can be judged on how well all stakeholders in both businesses benefit. If the merger leads to lower costs the shareholders may be happy, although less choice and therefore possibly higher prices may lead to a fall in the satisfaction of customers.

Although mergers and takeovers may lead to quicker growth and greater benefits in the long-run, the speed of growth created by this form of expansion may cause significant problems in the short-run. **(7–8 marks)**

examiner's tip	Evaluation requires you to weigh up the arguments from each side.

(c) *Knowledge*

Reasons may include:

- More personal service
- There are many niche markets in the holiday industry
- Few barriers to entry exist.

(1–2 marks)

Understanding/Application

- To set up as a travel agent requires minimal expense. A small office, a computer, a telephone & Internet link and some minimal advertising would allow any sole trader to set up in business.

- More-specialised holidays have a relatively low demand and so larger travel agents and tour operators would not be interested as they would not be able to offer such a service cost-effectively to such a small market segment.

(3–4 marks)

Analysis

The smaller travel firm may be catering for niche markets, e.g. coach holidays, holidays for walkers etc. The specialisation they can practise will provide for a more personalised service. There are limited opportunities for economies of scale in the industry because of the labour intensity. The recent growth in Internet holiday bookings has also allowed smaller firms to enter the market, as they do not even have the expense of an office or shop on the high street.   **(5–6 marks)**

---

(2) (a) *Knowledge*

As a business becomes bigger it is able to be more efficient, which should lead to more profits.   **(1–2 marks)**

Understanding/Application

- Nestlé will gain from economies of scale. This is where increased size leads to lower average fixed costs that lead to lower overall average costs.

- Nestlé will be able to purchase raw materials, such as cocoa, at a lower unit price because they are buying in greater bulk.   **(3–5 marks)**

Analysis

- Given that Nestlé has about 24% of the market according to the data in the case material, this will mean that they will have a dominant position in the market. Along with the other two 'big players', Cadbury and Mars, Nestlé are able to deter the arising of other smaller competitors, through barriers to entry.

- Nestlé's brand awareness will be very high because of their size. They will be able to spend vast amounts on promotion throughout Europe so that consumers are more likely to purchase their products.   **(6–8 marks)**

Evaluation

- However, Nestlé must have gained their current market position via an effective strategy of growth, including a merger with Rowntree Mackintosh. This will have required effective management and control of all resources, including employees, plant and machinery.

- Ultimately, the size of the business will have enabled Nestlé to be in a position to purchase other smaller competitors, introduce new products and pay for the best promotion and advertising available.   **(9–12 marks)**

(b) *Knowledge*

Multinationals provide jobs, new facilities and increased levels of technology for the host country. **(1–2 marks)**

Understanding/Application

- The injection of income into the economy that comes from increased employment will lead to long-term benefits as more money is being spent so leading to even more growth in the host economy.

- The introduction of large business into third world countries can lead to higher levels of pollution and exploitation of the workforce. Nike, for example, has been found to be using child labour and very cheap labour in less developed countries. **(3–5 marks)**

Analysis

- The benefits achieved by the creation of extra jobs will allow the host country to gain an improved economic position. Without the influence of multinationals it can be argued that the third world country would be unable to catch up with the developing world, leading to continued reliance on borrowing to enable their population to see an improvement in their standard of living.

- However, the problems listed in the second article highlight some of the less acceptable consequences of introducing multinationals into less developed countries. The health problems created by mothers using artificial baby milk will create long-term health issues for the host country and may lead to a forced change in the established culture of the country.

- It could be argued that Nestlé are acting unethically in gaining a foothold in the host country's market. Given the huge potential for growth in these countries, companies such as Nestlé are potentially taking advantage of the current low-income levels by providing the free baby milk in hospitals. **(6–8 marks)**

Evaluation

- The overall impact of multinationals such as Nestlé on host countries is difficult to judge. The increased incomes that come from the jobs created may be insignificant in the long-run given the increased dependence that these countries will have on multinationals in the future. Any extra income being earned is having to be used to buy the relatively more expensive products that the locals have become reliant on.

- It is impossible to know how the countries in question would have developed without the intervention of multinationals. It is also difficult to know who to believe. Nestlé state that they work closely with different organisations to ensure fairness – but fairness to whom? Those supporters of boycotts against Nestlé products would disagree about the sincerity of Nestlé's desire to be fair. **(9–12 marks)**

Chapter 3

Business objectives, planning and strategy

Questions with model answers

C grade candidate – mark scored 10/20

(a) How useful is the Boston Matrix in helping businesses analyse their product portfolio? [8]

(b) 'According to the theory of the Boston Matrix single product firms are unlikely to be successful in the long run.'
Evaluate this statement. [12]

[WJEC Specimen paper BS4]

?

For help see Revise A2 Study Guide sections 3.1 and 5.1

(a) The Boston Matrix or 'Boston Box' sets out to analyse a company's products under four headings: cash cows, stars, dogs, problem children.

The Boston Matrix shows visually where the firm stands with its products. Lots of 'dogs' means it should probably drop these products as soon as possible so that it can use the resources elsewhere. Lots of 'stars' means it must make sure they are kept and developed, to turn into 'cash cows'.

The Matrix doesn't take everything into account: for example, competitor actions. It won't therefore answer all the firm's questions to do with the range of products it sells.

(b) A single-product firm is just that: it makes and sells a single product. It may be doing this successfully – for example, in a niche market. A 'niche market' is one where the firm concentrates on just one market segment. Although this can be profitable, the firm is taking a lot of risks. For example, the niche market may collapse due to the actions of a government or a competitor, and people simply change tastes or fashion. If the firm relies on a single product, it will become bankrupt.

The Boston Box is designed for firms with more than one product, so it is of no real use to the single-product firm.

A good start, but the candidate then fails to explain either the purpose of the Matrix or its constituent elements.

The candidate makes a relevant point regarding the limitations of the Matrix, but then doesn't follow this up. You won't score many marks for a limited explanation and analysis such as this.

The candidate has described satisfactorily the difficulties that a single-product firm may find itself in, but has not provided any reasonable explanation of how the single-product firm can use the Matrix to analyse its product.

GRADE BOOSTER

Don't miss out on 'easy' marks by failing to explain your points in detail, which is a weakness in this candidate's answer.

Examiner's Commentary

(a) The Boston Matrix is a product portfolio analysis technique. It analyses products under four headings, showing the market share of each product and the rate of growth for the markets in which they are sold. This is the appearance of the 'Box'.

'Stars' are potentially highly profitable products, and heavy investment should convert them into 'cash cows', the key to the firm's profits and sales. 'Problem children' are also known as 'question marks', and serve the purpose of plugging a hole in the firm's product range. 'Dogs' are the unprofitable products that are also major users of the firm's resources.

Once the firm's product portfolio has been analysed using the Matrix, the marketing department can decide on its marketing strategies. If, for example, most products have been classified as 'cash cows', this suggests that the firm needs to start concentrating on new product development to maintain growth in the future. The limitations of the Matrix are, first, that it remains only a planning tool and will not decide the firm's marketing strategy on its own; second, placing products under the various headings can sometimes be difficult (e.g. as a result of limited market information); third, there are many relevant features of a product that are not taken into account by the Matrix.

This is an important paragraph: the candidate uses an example to analyse the relevance of the Matrix, and then balances this by considering its limitations. This brings evaluation into the answer.

The answer contains a diagram and explanation of the contents of the 'Box': this is a good idea so long as it doesn't dominate the answer, and it is supported by analysis and evaluation, as is the case here.

(b) The main benefit of using the Boston Matrix is that it encourages firms to examine the breadth of their product portfolio. It therefore most obviously relates to a large multi-product firm having a substantial product portfolio. The Matrix may still be useful to a single-product firm, however. The well-known problem that any single-product firm faces is having 'all its eggs in one basket': if there is a major change in market demand, e.g. due to some innovation or technological development by a competitor, the single-product firm can find it difficult to respond.

But a single-product firm may still have 'different' products. If only one product is being manufactured by a firm, it may still feature in more than one part of the 'Box': for example, if the firm exports the product as well as selling it in the UK. In the UK market, for example, it may be a 'cash cow', whereas in another market, such as Germany, it could be a 'star'. Product differentiation can also exist in the same market, e.g. through the firm adopting differentiated pricing policies or otherwise concentrating on a unique selling point of the product with one segment of its market. Some firms actively pursue, and are content with, a niche marketing position, making a single product and surviving profitably in this niche market.

The Boston Matrix still has a role to play for a single-product firm, and the firm may well survive in the long run if it is able to differentiate its product in some way, or use market segmentation effectively.

This is well related to the case study situation. We are only given a limited amount of information – 'single product firms' – so it becomes important to analyse what 'single product' can mean. The candidate does this well in this answer.

There is an assumption that a single product appears in just one section of the Matrix: this answer points out that this may not necessarily be so.

Exam practice questions

1 Natalie buys and sells paintings as a sole trader. She owns two shops, and employs two people in each shop. In order to optimise the selling and storage space in the shops, Natalie is considering also trading in antique furniture.

Natalie has been offered two antique items – a wardrobe, and a chair – by one of her customers. She has the chance to re-sell these items to a client overseas, where there is a high demand for these items. Natalie believes there is a 70% chance of making a £5000 profit if the overseas client will buy the wardrobe: if not, she faces a £2000 loss by having to store, advertise and sell it on the home market. With the chair, Natalie believes she has a 50% chance of a £10 000 profit by selling to the overseas client, or she will face a £5000 loss. The client can only afford to buy one of these items.

(a) **(i)** With the aid of a decision tree, evaluate the choices open to Natalie. [8]

(ii) Assess the value of decision trees as a way for Natalie to analyse business problems. [8]

Natalie wishes to appoint an assistant manager, to help with the proposed move to trading in antique furniture. She will either appoint by promoting someone from her present staff and then employ a replacement, or she will appoint the assistant manager from outside the business.

(b) Assess the effect of employment law on Natalie's recruitment and selection of an assistant manager. [12]

[Edexcel January 2002]

---

2 **(a)** Explain why the interests of a community might differ from those of businesses located within it. [8]

(b) Discuss the view that profits are more important to businesses than satisfying the interests of the community in which they are located. [12]

[WJEC January 2002]

Answers

(1) (a) **(i)** *Knowledge* and *Application/Understanding*

- Wardrobe: (70% × £5000) – (30% × £2000) = £2900 positive expected value.
- Chair (50% × £10 000) – (50% × £5000) = £2500 positive expected value.

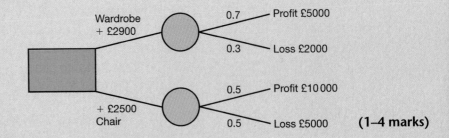

Wardrobe
+ £2900

0.7 — Profit £5000

0.3 — Loss £2000

+ £2500
Chair

0.5 — Profit £10 000

0.5 — Loss £5000 **(1–4 marks)**

Analysis

- There is a third choice: 'do nothing', with a zero expected value.
- Based on the above calculations, the decision is that the wardrobe has the higher positive expected value, and Natalie should buy it to sell to the overseas client. **(5–6 marks)**

Evaluation

- Natalie may choose to sell the wardrobe but she needs to bear in mind that the probabilities are estimates only.
- She will therefore need to consider other relevant factors such as the marketability of these items in the home market. **(7–8 marks)**

examiner's tip **Remember that, when calculating and constructing decision trees, there is always the 'do nothing' option.**

(ii) *Knowledge*

- Decision trees encourage people to adopt a quantitative approach to making business decisions. **(1 mark)**

Application/Understanding

- Natalie can make an objective comparison about this sale, based on financial or other numerical data. **(2 marks)**

Analysis

- Decision tree analysis is suited to making short-term tactical decisions such as the one Natalie needs to make.
- However, Natalie must recognise that there are other non-quantitative factors to take into account, such as the importance of her overseas client to her future business. **(3–5 marks)**

Evaluation

- Natalie has quantified risks and expected values, and must therefore consider the accuracy or otherwise of these figures.

- Decision trees ignore the unpredictability of a business environment such as the one in which Natalie works.

- Natalie should therefore make a judgement that is based not only on the results of her decision tree calculations. **(6–8 marks)**

(b) *Knowledge*

- Employment law issues include matters such as equality of opportunity, employee protection and health and safety.

- Laws include the Race Relations and Sex Discrimination Acts. **(1–3 marks)**

Application/Understanding

- Employment law applies at various stages of recruitment and selection, even in a small firm such as the one Natalie owns.

- For example, when seeking to appoint, Natalie may decide to advertise externally. She must ensure that any advertisement does not discriminate, e.g. in favour of men over women. **(4–6 marks)**

Analysis

- Natalie's business is in the same position as other organisations as regards the effect of this legislation.

- However, some areas of employment law may not apply, e.g. the Disability Discrimination Act (too few employees). **(7–9 marks)**

Evaluation

- Natalie must also remember that, even if appointing internally, she will need to give all staff equal opportunity to apply.

- Natalie therefore needs to consider the effect of employment laws at all stages of recruitment and selection, regardless of how these stages are carried out and to whom they apply. **(10–12 marks)**

examiner's tip | **It is important to consider the size of Natalie's business, and to point out that employment law is likely to influence all stages of the recruitment process.**

(2) (a) *Knowledge*

- The local community is an important stakeholder group for a business.
- The community typically seeks to minimise noise and other pollution in the locality, and maximise the benefits (e.g. employment) it gains from having the business located there. **(1–2 marks)**

Application/Understanding

- Local communities often welcome being involved with businesses in making decisions that affect the locality.
- They are particularly interested in limiting potentially harmful effects of the business being located there: e.g. pollution, congestion.
- Whilst businesses try to respond positively, it may be unrealistic for the community to expect no negative impacts, e.g. because of the cost implications to the businesses.
- Businesses will balance these cost implications against the benefits of keeping the local community happy.
- The community is normally less concerned about costs and more about benefits: e.g. businesses may seek to shed labour to save cost, whereas the local community wants jobs to remain. **(3–8 marks)**

(b) *Knowledge* and *Application/Understanding*

- Private sector businesses often seek to maximise profits, since profit is the reward given to enterprise.
- Public sector businesses, and some other businesses in the private sector (e.g. charities), do not focus on profit maximisation. **(1–4 marks)**

Analysis

- The nature and type of business influences its relationship with the community.
- For example, a manufacturing business may affect the local community through its noise, pollution and transport.
- These and other businesses will still concentrate on making profits, but will also be aware of the effects they have on the community. **(5–8 marks)**

Evaluation

- In reality, few businesses will follow a profit-maximising policy to the exclusion of other objectives.
- If businesses choose to ignore the local community, they may find their profits adversely affected, e.g. through bad publicity or facing fines for pollution.
- Their success will be judged not only by their profitability, but also on the extent to which they meet the needs of their local community. **(9–12 marks)**

examiner's tip | The term 'business' normally refers to private and public sector organisations, so in your answer you should refer to both sectors, and comment on the relevance of profit to each.

Chapter 4

Corporate and organisational culture

Questions with model answers

MIS at McVeigh Engineering Ltd

Examiner's Commentary

McVeigh Engineering Ltd, a medium-sized family business, is concerned about the quantity and quality of information received by its managers at all levels. Its senior management team met last week to discuss the situation. The Managing Director was very worried by this discussion. It was reported at the meeting that the business had been disadvantaged because managers hadn't been given the appropriate information. As a result, the firm has decided to introduce a Management Information System which will be based around increased use of computer technology. All offices will be networked with up-to-date computer equipment and managers will have their own computer terminals on their desks.

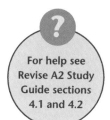

For help see Revise A2 Study Guide sections 4.1 and 4.2

(a) What is the purpose of a Management Information System? [8]

(b) Examine the issues which would have to be considered when designing an effective Management Information System for McVeigh Engineering Ltd. [10]

(c) Evaluate the impact on McVeigh Engineering Ltd of networking all its offices with up-to-date computer equipment and giving managers their own computer terminals on their desks. [12]

[CCEA 2000]

C grade candidate – mark scored 16/30

(a) Management needs information in order to help the firm survive. The management information system will provide this information so that managers can carry out their job of planning and controlling. Information from the management information system will therefore enable the firm to meets its stated objectives (e.g. market growth, increased profit).

The candidate should have started by clarifying the term used: this provides a focus for answering the question.

(b) With any new system, a business has to consider three main areas. First, its cost. The cost must be affordable to the business, otherwise the system will cost more than the value of the information it is giving to the management. Second, the people. The family here may have their own views about the type of system to be designed, and the designers will need to talk to them about this system.
Not only the family, but also all staff, some of whom will need a different sort of information, notably more detailed information to help them with their day-to-day work. Third, the structure of the business. A function-based business will have a hierarchy through which the information needs to pass. Designers will need to analyse this hierarchy, e.g. checking formal and informal lines of communication, in order to design an effective system.

Although the candidate has made three points, this answer is very general. There is little analysis of the case-study information, and limited reference only to the company. Compare this with how the A grade candidate starts the answer to this section.

(c) The positive side of the new system will be the speed and accuracy of what is produced, which seems to be needed by this business. It is likely that there will be an e-mail network within the business: this is quick and efficient, although sometimes it can be abused. The network may also have Internet access, which will enable managers to get a lot of information from outside the business. This is particularly helpful for managers in, say, marketing, where the information could be used for forecasting.

The downside of the system will obviously be its cost (see (b) above). Managers will need training in the use of this equipment, and it may be that some of them will resent having to use computers. Also, 'GIGO' – garbage in, garbage out – is associated with a computer-based information system.

There is no conclusion. Marks are often awarded for a conclusion where the candidate makes a judgement: here, no judgement has been made.

GRADE BOOSTER

Questions include information to make use of. To reach the higher grades, read the question carefully and make appropriate use of any information given.

A grade candidate – mark scored 28/30

(a) The main roles of managers are to take decisions, and to plan, co-ordinate and control their firm. Information is needed by managers and other staff for these purposes, but this information normally first arrives in the firm in the form of unstructured data. Examples include information from various sources about the firm's sales, paperwork to do with buying (e.g. invoices, orders), production figures, and so on. A management information system (MIS) sets out to change the data the firm has received into meaningful information. The MIS then uses a suitable format (e.g. number, text or diagrams; electronic or paper) to transmit this information to managers and others requiring it. The key purpose of MIS is therefore to provide information for decision-making. ←

> To save valuable writing time, using a well-known and popular abbreviation like 'MIS' is acceptable, but still include in your answer at least one reference to the full description.

(b) What we are told about the firm is that McVeigh Engineering Ltd is a medium-sized family business. As an engineering company it is likely to be involved in manufacturing, and could well be function-based (Production, Purchasing, Accounts, etc.). As a 'medium-sized' company, it will probably have some form of hierarchy and chain of command. Since it is a 'family' business, it has probably grown from being a small business: the family are still in control, but the company's culture and their management style isn't clear. One of the first tasks the designers have is to analyse the company's structure, culture and management style, because how the company is run will influence the design of the MIS. For example, different managers at different levels will require different amounts and types of information (e.g. 'strategic' and 'tactical' information). ←

> Notice how this candidate has studied carefully, and used, the information given. Suitable assumptions have been made and described: for example, the reference to the likely activity and structure of the company in the question.

Related to this will be any proposed changes in organisation and structure, which the designers will have to take account of. The crucial area for them is the nature of the information in the company: its sources, how it 'flows' through the hierarchy, how it is collected, stored, organised and transmitted.

The designers will also concentrate on the people currently employed: in particular, their existing computer skills and their feelings about a computer-based information system. The final influence here will be the cost of the system. The company isn't a large plc, its funds may well be limited, and this could limit the extent of the MIS. ←

> This is a thorough and well-explained analysis of the case-study information.

Corporate and organisational culture

Corporate and organisational culture

(c) It is clear from the question that the present level of information (quantity and quality) is not sufficient for the managers. If a computerised MIS is introduced, managers will gain as follows.

Communication should be faster: e.g. the network will offer e-mail facilities. Information will be able to be manipulated more easily: examples include the use of spreadsheets, possibly for budgeting or forecasting, or calculating ratios, and databases for the various customers and suppliers. This information will support the credit control system (e.g. by identifying and analysing 'aged' debtors), and again improve communication, e.g. by using the computer system to generate paperwork such as invoices. The company could also use dedicated software such as an accounting package to support this. Since the company is in engineering, managers may use other specialist software, e.g. CAD/CAM (computer-aided design and manufacture). From a marketing point of view, perhaps the company could get a presence on the Internet, to promote itself: access to the Internet will also help it obtain much more information (e.g. about competitors, or government statistics).

Overall, therefore, the company's data should be turned into meaningful information more easily, more quickly and more efficiently.

The problems the company may face include having to train managers and other employees in the use of this computer-based system. Many people are still uncomfortable with using computers, and there would also be a cost factor in having to take people away from their jobs for training. Second, computer hardware and software can date very quickly, so there is another cost-based issue, that of having to keep this system up-to-date (extra training would then be required, again costly). Finally, the company will probably have to meet the requirements of the 1998 Data Protection Act in terms of registration and disclosure of information, which adds to the administration required.

Overall, however, it seems that the advantages of such a MIS outweigh the disadvantages, especially since the cost of the system is likely to be exceeded by the benefits accruing from it.

Exam practice questions

1 R H Multimedia plc operates in a highly competitive and fast-changing environment. It employs 240 workers and has plants at three different locations. The firm is organised on a hierarchical structure with little worker participation. This probably arose as the firm has grown organically and is still largely owned and run by its founders.

However, changes are just around the corner. R H Multimedia plc has decided to introduce a flatter organisational structure with fewer levels of management and more employee empowerment.

(a) Suggest reasons for any business having to make changes. [8]

(b) Discuss:

    (i) the reasons why there may be resistance to change amongst the employees of R H Multimedia plc, and [4]

    (ii) ways in which management could minimise this resistance. [6]

(c) Evaluate R H Multimedia's decision to introduce a flatter organisational structure with fewer levels of management and more employee empowerment. [12]

[CCEA 2000]

---

2 **(a)** Describe ways in which corporate culture varies between different organisations. [8]

(b) Evaluate the view that a clear corporate culture is essential to the success of a business. [12]

[WJEC Summer 2002]

Answers on pages 40–42 Answers on pages 40–42 Answers on pages 40–42

Answers

(1) (a) *Knowledge*

- A business needs to stay competitive, and may have to improve its competitive position. It needs to react to competitors' moves, such as the introduction of a new competing model.

- There may also be technological advances that the business needs to incorporate into its work: if it fails to do so, its cost structure is likely to be less efficient than that of the competition.

- The business also needs to respond to changes in demand for its products: consumers' tastes change, and there are continuing demographic changes that may also affect the level of demand.

- Government legislation and other regulation changes, forcing the firm to review and if necessary change its practices (e.g. on employing people declaring a disability, on storing electronically data about customers, etc.).

(1–8 marks)

examiner's tip | The question asks for 'any business' so there is no need to base your comments on the business in the question.

(b) (i) *Knowledge*

- Many people resist change naturally.

- This may be due to the attitude 'things are fine as they are', or there may be other reasons such as the fear of job loss or of an inability to cope with the proposed change. **(1–2 marks)**

Application/Understanding

- The evidence of 'little worker participation' suggests that the R H Multimedia management has probably not consulted staff about proposed changes.

- The fact that the company is based in three locations adds to the difficulty of communicating with employees.

- This lack of communication is an important factor as to why change may be resented. **(3–4 marks)**

examiner's tip | Now you need to draw upon information in the question. Key quotes can be included, as illustrated above.

(b) (ii) *Knowledge* and *Application/Understanding*

- A full and immediate involvement with the policy of change is important: staff should be informed and consulted at all stages.

- The change should be introduced gradually, and linked with appropriate training for staff. **(1–3 marks)**

Analysis

- Involving staff means they will probably be less resistant to change as a result of knowing what is going on and why, and how they as individuals and as a group will be affected.

- It also helps them recognise the need for change, and to accept that in the longer term – e.g. job prospects through the firm surviving and growing – change is beneficial.

- Introducing change gradually will help the company liaise with unions and other staff organisations, which in turn will further motivate and please staff. **(4–6 marks)**

(c) *Knowledge* and *Application/Understanding*

- R H Multimedia operates in 'a highly competitive and fast changing environment'.

- With the pace of change, and the need to respond rapidly to this change, the company must be structured in such a way as to meet this challenge. **(1–2 marks)**

Analysis

- Flatter structures are associated with quicker decision-making, and with quicker response to customer needs and requirements, which will benefit R H Multimedia.

- Employee empowerment usually increases motivation, since staff are more involved in decisions and more responsible for their own actions.

- It is also often associated with greater financial incentives, better career paths, and greater promotional opportunities. **(3–6 marks)**

Evaluation

- One drawback associated with flatter structures is the increased spans of control that result.

- This may mean that a manager finds it difficult to exert proper control.

- Changes in job structure and operation can also cause conflict, and not everyone welcomes greater empowerment.

- If changes demotivate some staff, this could result in greater absenteeism and a higher labour turnover.

- Overall, the decision should benefit the company and its employees, through allowing it to respond more quickly and effectively to changes in its environment. **(7–12 marks)**

examiner's tip	Questions such as this may suggest a oversimplified answer: for example, 'Flatter structures are good, taller structures are bad'. However, a well-balanced answer must consider relevant drawbacks, even where one alternative (here, flatter structures) is sometimes simplified as always being 'better'.

(2) (a) *Knowledge*

- The term 'corporate culture' refers to the current dominant attitudes and ways of behaving in a business.

- The ideal corporate culture encourages all staff to support the business in appropriate ways. **(1–4 marks)**

Application/Understanding

- Cultures differ from business to business, depending for example on the attitudes and business philosophies of the owners, the business structure (e.g. 'tall' or 'flat'), or on the type of industry in which it is based.

- One difference is whether the business has a formal or informal culture, illustrated by (e.g.) use of first names and acceptability of certain types of dress/appearance.
- Cultures are also sometimes grouped under four headings: power culture, role culture, task culture and person culture. Each culture has its own features, advantages and disadvantages.
- For example, the power culture is often associated with small organisations that rely on a central source of power (the entrepreneur), whereas role cultures exist in organisations structured by function or specialism.
- Task cultures are associated with matrix structures, and person cultures are typical of small professional organisations. **(5–8 marks)**

examiner's tip | **In your answer, you can tackle 'different organisations' in several ways: for example, by size, by industry or by type of sector (public or private; primary, secondary or tertiary).**

(b) *Knowledge* and *Application/Understanding*
- Any business will have some form of corporate or organisational culture.
- Sometimes this culture may not be under the control of the managers. **(1–2 marks)**

Analysis
- A clear corporate culture is regarded as essential for many reasons.
- Managers can exert greater control when the culture is clear to all.
- They can then continue to shape this culture, e.g. through their communication and motivation strategies.
- Staff will identify more clearly with the business, and will also work more effectively in teams. **(3–6 marks)**

Evaluation
- However, there can sometimes be a 'culture gap' or 'culture clash'.
- A business with an unsuitable culture for its employees is likely to suffer from low levels of motivation, and potential conflict between managers and staff.
- Managers may also be reluctant to introduce change.
- In conclusion, it is necessary for managers to establish not only a clear culture, but also a culture that is acceptable to the majority of staff.
- By doing so, staff become aware of this culture and will follow it in order to help achieve the business's objectives. **(7–12 marks)**

examiner's tip | **This question also leaves it up to you as to whether or not you include examples of real businesses in your answer: it is often useful to do so.**

Chapter 5

Marketing

Questions with model answers

Gillette and the Mach 3

Gillette has launched its new razor – the Mach 3. This is the company's biggest and most important new product for eight years, but will it be successful? Gillette has 71% of the North American and European market for razors and blades but investors have begun to worry about slowing growth, partly due to a smaller rival recently launching a new razor of its own.

Eight years ago Gillette was losing its grip on the razor market to cheap throwaways and facing yet another hostile take-over bid. Its new product at that time, the Sensor razor, saved the firm and today it is vastly stronger, being one of America's 30 biggest companies. The company also owns such brand names as Duracell batteries and Parker pens.

The Mach 3 razor will test Gillette's unusual approach to innovation in the consumer products business. Most companies produce in response to competition or demand but Gillette boasts that it launches a new product only when it has made a genuine technical advance. An example is the Duracell Ultra battery which is designed to last 50% longer than its rivals and is specially designed for palmtop computers and personal CD players which need and use a great deal of power. It is also priced at 20% more than a conventional battery. Gillette spends 2.2% of its turnover on research and development: that is twice as much as the average consumer products company.

Three-quarters of the money spent on the Mach 3 razor has gone on 200 new pieces of specialist machinery, designed in-house, which will churn out 600 new razor blade cartridges per minute, tripling the current speed of production. This means that the investment will pay for itself within two years. The fact that the company spends more on new production equipment than on new products is one reason why Gillette regularly hits its target of reducing manufacturing costs by 4% per year.

Another difference between Gillette and most other consumer product companies is that it does not tailor its products to local tastes. This gives it vast economies of scale in manufacturing. Gillette's products obviously have global appeal. Last year 70% of its sales were outside America. More than 1.2 billion people now use at least one of its products every day. The company has 91% of the market for blades in Latin America and 69% in India.

Source: © the *Economist,* London, 18 April, 1998

(a) Explain the phases of development through which the firm's new Mach 3 razor is likely to have been taken. [6]

(b) Discuss the factors that Gillette may have considered when designing its new razor. [10]

(c) Evaluate the impact on Gillette of spending so much of its turnover on research and development that is not in direct response to competition or demand. [14]

[CCEA Specimen]

For help see Revise A2 Study Guide sections 5.3 and 8.2

C grade candidate – mark scored 15/30

(a) The phases start with collecting and sifting through new ideas. Once this is done, the firm starts looking at the likely success of the product. It will test-market it to gauge consumer reaction. If all goes well, the product will be launched.

> The phases between evaluating the idea and test-marketing the product have been omitted, and there is no application of this knowledge to the Mach 3 razor.

(b) The designers will need to consider the razor's costs when designing it: the razor can't be too expensive, otherwise the company will not make a profit on it. How it is going to be made will also influence design: it must be capable of being made efficiently and easily, so the finished product is workable. Lastly, the razor should be designed with a USP (unique selling point) in mind if at all possible, to differentiate it from all the other razors on sale.

> Terms such as 'workable' are rather vague, and should be clarified. Although this answer relates to the given product, it lacks the organisation and structure of the A grade one.

(c) Research and development is not guaranteed to give a company a return, but there is plenty of evidence that Gillette is doing well from its own research and development. Gillette is obviously very successful, judging by its market share in its various markets. This is partly due to research and development leading to new technology, and better production processes – e.g. the specialist machinery can triple the current speed of production. It has also helped Gillette produce other products that show a technological advance, e.g. the Duracell battery. In doing so, Gillette can stay ahead of the market, and lead rather than follow. Financially, it can offset the 4% savings in manufacturing costs against the 2.2% cost of research and development, which shows it is well worthwhile for Gillette to invest in this research and to develop new products.

> Even given the strength of evidence that R&D is benefiting Gillette, the candidate should still have presented evidence of the negative impacts of R&D expenditure.

GRADE BOOSTER

This is potentially a very good answer, but it lacks the depth of explanation you will see in the A grade answer. Examiners can often award as many marks to detailed explanations of one or two points as they will to brief answers that outline many points.

A grade candidate – mark scored 29/30

(a) The normal stages of new product development, which apply to the Mach 3, include the following. First, new ideas for razors are obtained and then evaluated, to ensure good ideas are not rejected. A prototype razor is then created and tested, to check likely market reaction (e.g. demand level) as well as the expected cost to see if it is financially viable. The razor's design is then finalised, the razor developed, and test-marketed. This takes place to assess whether the razor's target market (adult males) will react favourably to it. The razor is then officially launched, and starts its 'life' in terms of the product life-cycle.

> The stages are not just listed: there is also some description and explanation where required, all in the context of the Mach 3 razor.

(b) When designing a razor, Gillette's design team must have paid careful attention to safety requirements. Since Gillette exports its razors to many countries, it will need to be aware of safety regulations not only in the USA, but in its other markets (e.g. the EU countries). Related to this are consumer expectations of reliability: the razor will need to be reliable in order to be safe and to encourage repeat purchases. The design team will also have wanted to design a razor that is pleasing to the eye (e.g. suitable use of colour in materials), but, even more importantly, one that is functional. To be 'functional', a razor must be comfortable to handle and easy to use.

> There is effective use of the information given, in particular the nature of the product. 'Theory' is also linked well to the given situation.

The design team will work closely with three business functions in particular. First, production: the razor should be easy to produce, making use if possible of existing equipment and staff skills. Second, accounts: the razor must be capable of making a profit, so the design team will also have to bear in mind the financial implications of their design. Finally, marketing: the marketing department will be looking for a design that helps the marketing of the new razor: issues such as display and storage will therefore be considered by the design team.

> This is a well-organised and analysed answer. Notice how the candidate identifies relevant business functions, and relates design points to these functions.

(c) There is plenty of evidence of a positive impact on Gillette as a result of its relatively high spending on research and development (R&D). The case study mentions that Gillette has 71% of the North American and European razor market, and substantial sections of other markets: the company will need to invest heavily in R&D due to the nature of its global market. Gillette is a proactive company rather than a reactive one, because it seeks new technological development, and it also leads rather than having to respond to competitors' developments and initiatives. The technology it gains from its R&D can probably be used to improve the production of its other products: the evidence is in reaching its target of a 4% cut each year in its manufacturing costs. The investment in new technology resulting from R&D also has a quick payback period (a 2-year period is stated). Also, by developing 'in-house' Gillette becomes less reliant on outside suppliers, and is therefore in greater control of its own destiny.

> The candidate also uses production and financial terms and ideas effectively. Although the question focuses on research and development, the candidate is (correctly) using terms and ideas from both Production and Finance to good effect. Again, information given in the question, such as the payback period of the investment, is included appropriately here.

The risk remains that such a heavy expenditure on R&D may result in the company producing a product that isn't demanded. There is also evidence that investment in R&D may not always yield the right answers or the right technology (e.g. when Gillette was hit badly by the development of competitors' cheap, throwaway razors). Overall, however, Gillette seems to be profiting from this major investment.

> This answer draws effectively on the evidence presented in the case study.

Marketing

Exam practice questions

1 Chocalot Ltd is a manufacturer of a small but expensive range of chocolate confectionery. Sales in recent years have varied considerably. The peak sales period is usually the run-up to Christmas and sales are at their lowest during the summer months. The directors are planning to expand the company's capacity and have already attempted to increase sales at other times of the year. They are anxious to establish the seasonal variation in sales and to forecast future sales levels. The following data relates to sales in recent years:

Year	Quarter	Sales (£000)	4 quarter moving average
1997	3	130	
	4	128	
1998	1	118	132.75
	2	155	131.50
	3	125	134.50
	4	140	138.00
1999	1	132	136.75
	2	150	137.25
	3	127	137.25
	4	140	134.25
2000	1	120	

Quarterly Sales Figures

(a) Using the four quarter moving average calculation given, centre the results using an appropriate method on the insert provided and from this show the predicted trend value for sales for quarter 2 in 2000. **[8]**

(b) Using your results, calculate the average seasonal variation for the second quarter. **[4]**

(c) In the light of your results, assess the company's intentions to raise its capacity and to try to increase sales. **[5]**

(d) Evaluate the appropriateness of time-series analysis as a method of forecasting sales for a business operating in a luxury product market. **[8]**

[Edexcel 2000]

2 (a) Explain the importance of market research in the development of a marketing strategy for a new product. **[8]**

(b) Discuss how the marketing strategy of a soap manufacturer might differ from that of a car manufacturer. **[12]**

[WJEC Specimen]

Answers on pages 47–49 Answers on pages 47–49 Answers on pages 47–49

Answers

(1) (a) *Knowledge and Application*

1997	3	
	4	
		132.75
1998	1	132.125
		131.50
	2	133.00
		134.50
	3	136.25
		138.00
	4	137.375
		136.75
1999	1	137.00
		137.25
	2	137.25
		137.25
	3	135.75
		134.25
	4	
2000	1	

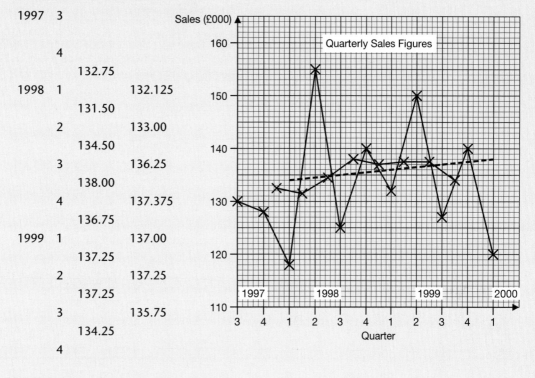

Sales (£000) — Quarterly Sales Figures — Quarter — 1997 1998 1999 2000

- Estimated trend value for 2000 quarter 2 = 141.5 **(1–8 marks)**

(b) *Application/Understanding*

- Average seasonal variation for quarter 2 is:
  (1998) Actual 155 less 133 = +22
  (1999) Actual 150 less 137.25 = +12.75
- Overall average = (+22 and +12.75 divided by 2) + 17.375 **(1–4 marks)**

(c) *Knowledge* and *Application/Understanding*

- The trend suggests that there is a steady, but not dramatic, underlying increase in the company's sales. **(1–2 marks)**

Analysis

- The sales figures suggest that there is sufficient capacity existing to increase sales at other times of the year. **(3–4 marks)**

Evaluation

- Although there is an underlying increasing trend, there are no clear patterns of growth in each quarter, however: each quarter shows fluctuating sales from year to year.
- The company may therefore seek to promote sales of its chocolates, especially at other times of the year. **(5 marks)**

(d) *Knowledge*

- In general, time series analysis depends on the reliability of the data used, provides a purely quantitative analysis, and also ignores random external variations (the unpredictable element). **(1–2 marks)**

Application/Understanding

- Chocalot Ltd can use time series analysis, since it has data collected, and there is evidence that its sales are seasonal. **(3–4 marks)**

Analysis

- Time series analysis may be of greatest use in the short term, and is based on the assumption that history repeats itself.

- The evidence Chocalot Ltd has suggests this doesn't happen in its market, since there is a reference that 'Sales in recent years have varied considerably'. **(5–6 marks)**

Evaluation

- Time series may be better suited to a mass market analysis, since the luxury chocolate market may not provide adequate or suitable data for analysis.

- Also, it may be subject to major unpredictable occurrences (e.g. health scares for chocolate). **(7–8 marks)**

---

(2) (a) *Knowledge*

- 'Market research' involves obtaining primary and/or secondary data about the market for a product: e.g. consumer lifestyles, ages, buying habits, etc.

- 'Marketing strategy' refers to a business plan that will enable the firm to meet its stated marketing objectives.

- The strategy will consider elements of marketing such as the marketing mix, the product portfolio and its analysis, as well as the results of using techniques such as SWOT analysis. **(1–4 marks)**

Application/Understanding

- In developing a marketing strategy there will be a need to identify customers' needs in the market or segment that is being targeted, the nature and degree of competition, market trends, pricing patterns, and so on.

- Some of this information can be obtained through market research, which may be quantitative and/or qualitative in nature.

- For example, buyer behaviour could be determined through surveys or observation, and competitor policies and performance through statistical analysis.

- This evidence will contribute towards developing a medium- to long-term strategy. **(5–8 marks)**

(b) *Knowledge* and *Application/Understanding*

- There are differences and similarities between the markets for soap and for cars.
- Both are 'mass' markets, both are at home and abroad, although different cultures, tastes and regulations (e.g. right-hand or left-hand drive; the acceptance of scented soaps) mean that these markets need researching carefully by both manufacturers. **(1–2 marks)**

Analysis

- Although cars are thought of more as a 'luxury' and soap as a 'necessity', there are different segments in both markets (e.g. small hatchback/'second car' market compared with performance car market; everyday toilet soaps compared with luxury 'gift' soaps).
- As a result, both manufacturers' strategies will need to consider the relevant segment(s) in which the firm will sell, develop or enter, as well as the differing needs of consumers. **(3–6 marks)**

Evaluation

- The soap and car markets differ in terms of the degree and type of competition.
- Both car and soap markets currently feature few producers who are often selling relatively similar products, so non-price promotion and competition are likely to be important features of the firms' strategies.
- The strategy for both manufacturers will probably try to identify some USP feature of their products, which is likely to be easier for the car manufacturer.
- Both strategies will probably feature persuasive and informative advertising, e.g. concentrating on the 'youthful' appeal of soap or some style/image feature for cars. **(7–12 marks)**

| examiner's tip | You are given clear guidelines here, and so must relate as many points as possible to the two types of manufacturers identified in the question. When asked about how something might 'differ', remember to present points outlining similarities as well as differences. |

Chapter 6

Accounting and finance

Questions with model answers

Decision-making at Turner and Turner Ltd

Turner & Turner Limited makes lawn mowers. Most of the work is concerned with producing large grass cutters on which the operator can ride. Three models are made and the company also has a repairs and spares department. The engines are brought in from an overseas manufacturer and fitted to the mower that the company makes itself.

The company presently uses a full costing method but there are plans to cease production of the least profitable model. The following criteria will be used to allocate the overheads:

- Rent and rates will be allocated according to the number of machines sold;
- Power costs will be allocated according to the cost of direct labour;
- Administration costs will be split equally between the three models.

The selling price of each model and direct costs of production are shown below:

	Model A £	Model B £	Model C £
Selling price	2000	2800	3600
Direct materials	400	500	600
Direct labour	800	1000	1400
Engine	600	700	900
Units sold/year	80	120	200

The figures below show the overhead costs faced by the company.

	£000
Rent & rates	128
Power	16
Administration	39

(a) Using the proposed absorption costing method, calculate the total profits generated by each of the three models for the business. [6]

(b) Using the information available, calculate the contribution from each model. [3]

(c) Assess the consequences of the plan to cease production of the least profitable model. [8]

(d) The firm has been approached to supply 50 Model C machines to an overseas buyer. What advice on pricing the order would you give the firm? [8]

[Edexcel 2000]

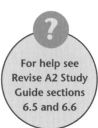

For help see Revise A2 Study Guide sections 6.5 and 6.6

Examiner's Commentary

(a) Model:

	A (£)	B (£)	C (£)
Unit sales revenue	2 000	2800	3600
Unit direct costs	1800	2200	2900
Unit contribution	200	600	700
Number sold	80	120	200
Total contribution	16 000	72 000	140 000
Less overheads:			
rent & rates	25 600	38 400	64 000
power	4 000	5 000	7 000
administration	13 000	13 000	13 000
Profits	(26 600)	15 600	56 000

This display shows contribution, because here the direct costs are variable and the overheads are fixed costs. The candidate has not apportioned the power costs correctly, wrongly using the unit direct labour figures rather than the total figures.

(b) Contribution is shown in (a) as
A = £16 000, B = £72 000, C = £140 000

(c) Model A is obviously the product making the biggest (the only) loss, so dropping it would save the company a lot of money. It loses £26 600 a year, so Turner & Turner will make a profit of £71 600, the profits for models B and C, if it is dropped.

The candidate doesn't realise that fixed costs will still have to be paid regardless of whether the company makes three, two or even no models. The profits for B and C can't simply be added together if A is dropped from the product range.

(d) Turner & Turner Ltd can sell its model C at a price of £3600. It will make extra profit, because all its costs have been paid by its current sales. Selling 200 of model C makes a profit of £56 000, so an additional 50 will add another £14 000 profit.

The candidate has made one relevant point, but the calculation of the additional profit is wrong: it isn't as simple as this!

Accounting and finance

GRADE BOOSTER

This candidate hasn't shown a full understanding of the nature of fixed and variable costs. A fuller understanding would have led to more accurate calculations and conclusions.

Examiner's Commentary

(a)

	A (£ 000)	B (£ 000)	C (£ 000)
Revenue	160	336	720
Direct costs:			
direct materials	32	60	120
direct labour	64	120	280
engines	48	84	180
Overheads:			
rent & rates	25.6	38.4	64
power	2.206	4.137	9.655
administration	13	13	13
Total costs	184.806	319.537	666.655
Profits	(24.806)	16.463	53.345

Calculations:

rent & rates = A $\dfrac{80 \times £128}{400}$ B $\dfrac{120 \times £128}{400}$ C $\dfrac{200 \times £128}{400}$

power: A £64 000 + B £120 000 + C 280 000 = £464 000 total direct labour

power = A $\dfrac{64 \times £16}{464}$ B $\dfrac{120 \times £16}{464}$ C $\dfrac{280 \times £16}{464}$

(b) The contribution from each model is:

	A (£)	B (£)	C (£)
Sales revenue	2 000	2 800	3 600
Direct (variable) costs	1 800	2 200	2 900
Unit contribution	200	600	700
Number sold	80	120	200
Total contribution	16 000	72 000	140 000

These calculations are not only accurate, but also well laid out. The candidate has also used an appropriate number of decimal places (representing hundreds, tens and units).

There are a lot of calculations for 6 marks, so make sure a suitable layout is used such as the one chosen here. Calculations are shown, which is important.

Both unit and total contribution figures are shown. The tabular layout is both clear and time-saving, very important in an examination.

(c) The least profitable model is A, because using the absorption costing
     method it makes a loss of £24 806. It does, however, make a positive
     contribution to the fixed costs of £200 a unit, £16 000 on present sales. In
     this sense it is 'profitable', and the question should be asked: is the
     apportionment of the (fixed cost) overheads fair? For example, it seems
     unlikely that model A will take a third of the administration costs, because
     it only makes up 20% of sales volume (80 out of 400). The apportionment of
     rent and rates on numbers sold can also be queried. Turner & Turner Ltd ◄
     must also consider the opportunity cost of dropping A. If it is dropped, this
     may allow competitors to enter the market. Also, if A is dropped, can the
     company use the resources released more efficiently and profitably?

> The candidate has extracted and used calculations very effectively here, and has introduced an important relevant concept (opportunity cost).

(d) Assuming the company has spare capacity, it can afford to sell the
     50 model C products at any figure above £2900, which is the marginal cost
     for this model (the total direct costs). It can afford to do this because,
     at present sales levels, all fixed costs are covered by the contributions
     made by the three models. Therefore, any additional items sold will bring
     profit as long as their selling price is above their variable cost – in this
     case, £2900. The problem could be for Turner and Turner that, if it allows a
     'special low-price deal', other customers may discover this and demand ◄
     similar deals. If the company thinks this won't happen and it has spare
     productive capacity, it can decide on any price above the £2900 figure. If it
     decides to sell at £3600, it will make £700 profit on each item sold (£35 000
     in total).

> The candidate is well aware of the marginal costing arguments here. The points are well explained, and supported by relevant figures and calculations.

Accounting and finance

1 Oakbank Foods plc is one of Europe's leading manufacturers of convenience foods such as ready meals, pizza, cakes and desserts and sandwiches. It manufactures its products in the UK, Holland, Republic of Ireland, Germany and Portugal and employs over 11 000 people. The company has a clear objective of being European market leader in a range of convenience foods.

The following is an extract from the company's operational review for 1999.

'In the Republic of Ireland and on the Continent the transition to Euro trading has gone smoothly. However, the early weakness of the Euro has restrained any major growth in direct exports from the UK.'

Information taken from the company's accounts is shown below.

	1999 (millions)	1998 (millions)
Turnover	£788.9	£774.2
Cost of Sales	£633.4	£613.8
Gross Profit	£155.5	£160.4
Net Profit	£27.4	£48.1
Dividends Issued	£17.7	£16.9
Current Assets	£169.4	£203.2
Current Liabilities	£200.7	£167.0
Total Capital Employed	£228.8	£280.3

	1995	1996	1997	1998	1999
Gearing Ratio	85%	79%	51%	34%	42%
Dividend per share	6.7p	6.7p	6.9p	7.3p	7.6p
Earnings per share	9.4p	11.3p	11.9p	13.4p	13.7p

(a) Calculate, for 1998 and 1999, the following ratios for Oakbank Foods plc (give your answer correct to one decimal place):

  (i) return on capital employed

  (ii) net profit percentage. [6]

(b) Explain the extract from the company's operational review for 1999. [10]

(c) On the basis of the information in the case study, discuss whether or not a potential investor might be wise to invest in shares in Oakbank Foods plc. [14]

[CCEA Specimen]

Accounting and finance

2 Savelots Ltd is a successful retail shop in a large town. It sells a variety of foodstuffs and other products. Due to its success, the directors are planning to invest in a new electronic check-out system.

There are two systems available. One is sold for £40 000 by Sellwell Ltd, a local firm, and the other for £30 000 by No-Q plc, a company located some 300 km (200 miles) from Savelots Ltd. If a system is bought and installed, the expected gain in profits from improved efficiency is:

Year	Expected gain in profits (£) (Sellwell equipment)	Expected gain in profits (£) (No-Q equipment)
1	25 000	20 000
2	20 000	20 000
3	20 000	15 000
4	5 000	5 000

(a) Using **one** appropriate investment appraisal technique, analyse the alternatives available to Savelots Ltd. [8]

(b) Assess the extent to which investment appraisal techniques will provide full information for the directors of Savelots Ltd. [16]

[Edexcel Summer 2002]

3 Recently, there have been rumours concerning the financial position of Lee & Co, one of Savelots Ltd's suppliers. The summarised financial statements of Lee & Co are as follows:

Lee & Co
Profit & loss accounts for the year ended 31 December

	2001	2000
	£000	£000
Turnover	900	650
Cost of sales	550	355
Gross profit	350	295
Expenses	245	165
Net profit	105	130

Lee & Co
Balance sheets at 31 December

	2001		2000	
	£000	£000	£000	£000
Fixed assets		1725		989
Current assets	235		430	
Current liabilities	(192)		(202)	
Net current assets		43		228
Debenture loan		(750)		(250)
Net assets		1018		967
Ordinary share capital		600		600
Profit and loss account		418		367
		1 018		967

The industry average ratios are as follows:

	2001	2000
Gross profit percentage	44.2%	45.5%
Net profit percentage	21.1%	21.2%
Return on capital employed	10.2%	10.5%
Current ratio	1.7:1	1.8:1
Gearing	32%	30%

(a) Using the above financial information, evaluate whether the company should continue to use Lee & Co as a supplier. [20]

(b) Assess the value of accounting statements when judging the performance of a business such as Lee & Co. [16]

[Edexcel Summer 2002]

Answers

(1) (a) *Knowledge* and *Application/Understanding*

    (i) 1999 = (27.4 × 100)/228.8 = 12.0%
          1998 = (48.1 × 100)/280.3 = 17.2%

    (ii) 1999 = (27.4 × 100)/788.9 = 3.5%
          1998 = (48.1 × 100)/774.2 = 6.2%   **(1–6 marks)**

(b) *Knowledge*

- Reference to the Euro is to the single currency adopted in 12 EU countries (excluding the UK).
- The phrase 'transition to Euro trading has gone smoothly' refers to the use of the Euro as a trading currency.   **(1–2 marks)**

Application/Understanding

- Oakbank Foods, having factories in Holland, Ireland, Germany and Portugal, can use the Euro in its inter-country trading.
- Reference to 'early weakness of the Euro' refers to its trading value against other currencies, notably the pound and dollar.
- In the first two years of its existence, the Euro fell against these currencies but has since recovered.   **(3–6 marks)**

Analysis

- Because its factories are in Holland, Ireland, Germany and Portugal, Oakbank Foods will not be concerned with exchange rate fluctuations but will face greater price transparency.
- The value of the Euro and the £ affect Oakbank because exports measured in sterling will be relatively expensive, and imports relatively inexpensive. As a result, UK exports are affected ('restrained any major growth in direct exports from the UK').   **(7–10 marks)**

(c) *Knowledge* and *Application/Understanding*

- The figures suggest there are a number of arguments in favour of investing:
  - turnover;
  - dividends;
  - earnings per share.
- The figures also suggest a number of arguments against investing:
  - profitability;
  - net profit margin;
  - working capital ratio;
  - gearing.   **(1–4 marks)**

Analysis

- Turnover is increasing.
- There are higher dividends (over the five years dividend per share increased from 6.7p to 7.6p).
- Earnings per share have also increased (9.4p to 13.7p).
- However, there is reduced profitability – **(a)** shows falling net profit margin and return on capital employed.

- The net profit margin has fallen by more (2.7%) than gross profit margin (from 20.7% to 19.7% = 1% fall), indicating expenses as a % of turnover have increased (from 14.5% to 16.2%).

- The working capital ratio is now less than 1 (0.8) compared with 1.2 in 1998 – this indicates a worsening liquidity position.

- Gearing has also increased since 1998, although it is significantly lower than five years ago. **(5–10 marks)**

Evaluation

- The conclusion is that there are some concerns about the company's present levels of profitability and liquidity.

- More information is required.

- Some of this information could be obtained from copies of the company's full final accounts. **(11–14 marks)**

examiner's tip	Like many financial analysis questions, there isn't a simple answer. You need to concentrate on the key issues of profitability and liquidity.

(2) (a) *Knowledge* and *Application/Understanding*

- <u>Payback</u>
  - ○ Sellwell = $1\frac{3}{4}$ years (£25 000 year 1 + [£15 000/£20 000 × 1 year])
  - ○ No-Q = $1\frac{1}{2}$ years (£20 000 year 1 + [£10 000/£20 000 × 1 year])

- <u>Accounting (or Average) rate of return (ARR)</u>
  - ○ Sellwell £70 000/4 = average £17 500 profits:
  - ○ ARR = £17 500/£40 000 = 43.75% (44%)
  - ○ No-Q £60 000/4 = average £15 000 profits:
  - ○ ARR = £15 000/£30 000 = 50% **(1–4 marks)**

Analysis

Payback

- Payback for Sellwell takes three months longer than for No-Q.

- The payback calculations suggest a broadly similar risk, although Sellwell is slightly riskier due to the longer payback time.

ARR

- No-Q has a higher ARR of 50%, compared with 43.75%.

- There is a lower outlay for the No-Q system.

- Although profits are given, there is no guarantee they are equal to cash flow. **(5–8 marks)**

examiner's tip	Note that you are only asked to use *one* investment appraisal technique, so don't waste valuable exam time using two. Different formulae can be used to calculate ARR, and you would receive full credit for using any accepted formula.

(b) *Knowledge*

- The payback method shows how quickly the investment outlay is repaid.

- The ARR technique is used to assess the apparent profitability of the project.

(1–2 marks)

Application/Understanding

- The payback technique ignores the value of money, so on its own it provides an incomplete analysis for the directors.

- The ARR technique ignores cash payback and value of money, so this is also an incomplete analysis for the directors.

- Using discounted cash flow / net present value in addition to the above would give the directors a fuller picture. **(3–4 marks)**

Analysis

- The directors, especially in this case, must always consider the degree of accuracy of forecasts.

- The directors should also compare the expected return to the company's cost of capital. **(5–10 marks)**

Evaluation

- Additional information such as market conditions is needed before decisions about investing should be made.

- The directors should consider not only financial, but also non-financial, arguments.

- Examples of non-financial arguments include considering the level of customer satisfaction, the comparative quality of these two systems, and that No-Q is much further away than Sellwell (so the directors should consider servicing issues). **(11–16 marks)**

examiner's tip	Your answer needs to recognise that investment appraisal techniques should be used in conjunction with other information.

(3) (a) *Knowledge* and *Application/Understanding*

- Relevant calculations could include (% unless shown otherwise):

	2001	Lee	Industry	2000	Lee	Industry
Gross profit	350/900 =	**38.9**	**44**	295/650 =	**45.4**	**46**
Net profit	105/900 =	**11.7**	**20**	130/650 =	**20.0**	**21**
ROCE	105/1768 =	**5.9**	**10**	130/1217 =	**10.7**	**11**
(or ROCE)	105/1018 =	**10.3**	**10**	130/967 =	**13.4**	**11**
Current ratio	235/192 =	**1.2 to 1**	**2:1**	430/202 =	**2.1 to 1**	**2:1**
Gearing	750/1768 =	**42.4**	**32**	250/1217 =	**20.6**	**30**
(or Gearing)	750/1018 =	**73.7**	**32**	250/967 =	**25.9**	**30**

(1–6 marks)

Analysis

- In profitability terms, in 2000 Lee was close to the industry average for both gross and net profit margins, but there is evidence of a decline in 2001, and now Lee is well below the industry average.

- Lee's expenses as a percentage of turnover increased in 2001, from 25.4% to 27.2%.

- In 2000, Lee's return on capital employed was very close to the industry average, but is now much lower (**OR** in 2000 Lee's ROCE was above the industry average but it has now fallen to the same level).

- (In either case) this is largely due to the increased debentures.

- In terms of liquidity, Lee's current ratio has fallen from above the industry average in 2000 to well below it in 2001.

- This suggests Lee may soon face difficulty in meeting its debts.

- Lee's gearing was lower in 2000 than the industry average, but in 2001 is now much higher.

- This is due to the increase in debentures. **(7–12 marks)**

Evaluation

- The fall in Lee's profit margins in 2001 seem to be due to a sales drive or expansion.

- Turnover is up by 38–39%, but expenses are up by nearly 50%.

- Other evidence of expansion is the increased value of Lee's fixed assets.

- This expansion seems to be financed partly by debentures, and partly from Lee's current assets.

- But by using current assets for this purpose, Lee is reducing its liquidity.

- Lee also now faces higher debenture interest payments.

- In conclusion, it may be advisable for Savelots not to use Lee at present.

- Especially since fresh food is concerned (a reliable supplier is needed for perishable foodstuffs). **(13–20 marks)**

examiner's tip You can plan your analysis of the situation under, say, three headings: profitability, liquidity and gearing.

(b) *Knowledge* and *Application/Understanding*

- Accounting statements, such as the Profit & Loss Account and the Balance Sheet, can provide objective judgement about the financial position of businesses such as Lee & Co.

- These statements compare 'like with like', for example by calculating ratios from Lee's final accounts. **(1–6 marks)**

Analysis

- Financial statements will only give a 'snapshot' of Lee's financial situation.

- For example, the effect of Lee's price and other changes may or may not be reflected in the information.

- The financial information is historical and cost-based, and may not be the most appropriate to use in this context. **(7–10 marks)**

Evaluation

- Savelots cannot judge the quality of Lee's workforce, and other non-financial factors, just by studying the accounting statements.

- These statements will also not show Lee's risk profile, nor the impact of Lee's size and market share.

- Different firms may use different accounting policies, so any interfirm analysis of financial information in accounting statements is of limited value only.

- These statements will therefore give Savelots some valuable information about Lee's financial performance, but only give limited non-financial information. **(11–16 marks)**

| examiner's tip | The questions asks about company 'performance', which is not limited to financial performance only, so this needs acknowledging in your conclusion. |

Chapter 7

People in organisations

Questions with model answers

Bradley and Moores plc

Bradley and Moores plc operates throughout the UK, making and assembling office furniture. Its plant in Birmingham is the largest of nine production centres. The main changes that have taken place recently are linked to the spread of information technology and delayering. Last year, the whole company was reorganised to meet the requirements of ISO 9001. Not everyone was happy with these changes.

Chelsea Rimmer, the firm's legal adviser, was about to have a meeting with the Assistant Personnel Manager, Hugh Hurley. Hugh began by explaining that there had been a dismissal in the Marketing Department. 'One of the account managers, Mark, who has had some sort of viral infection for years was dismissed by the Marketing Manager. It was felt that Mark had been using his illness as an excuse for having excessive time off. Eventually we just could not cope with his repeated absences. The work was not getting done.'

Hugh also outlined a second problem: 'I have just been made aware by our Production Manager of an incident that happened last week with one of the company's long-serving maintenance workers, Bob Malone. Someone tripped over some tools he had left out whilst he had a coffee break and broke his arm. I have spoken to Bob before about his untidiness, but it's not really my job to monitor him; that should be done by his line manager.'

After listening carefully to these two stories, Chelsea looked concerned. 'I should have been made aware of these problems earlier. I have been worried about the number of accidents happening in this company for some time now.'

?

For help see Revise A2 Study Guide sections 7.2 and 7.5

(a) Suggest what possible action may be taken by Hugh Hurley to reduce the number of accidents at the plant. [10]

(b) Discuss how these two cases demonstrate the existence of communication problems at Bradley and Moores. [10]

(a) Accidents occur because there is not enough attention being paid to safe working. All companies must follow Health & Safety procedures and this company needs to follow the guidelines more closely. It may be better training that is needed. Workers may be unaware of the procedures to be followed, although we are told that Bob is a long-serving worker and so he should know better. Maybe he is not motivated enough. This can be improved by better pay or better conditions.

It may be that the managers are too busy to monitor all of the employees. We are told that the company has just gone through many changes for ISO 9001 and delayering. This may have led to greater demands on the management so that they have neglected some of their duties. It may be a good idea for the company to appoint a member of the company responsible for all safety issues.

Although this answer does well to highlight possible causes of the accidents, very little attention is made to solving them, which is what the question is primarily about.

(b) The Marketing Manager should not be dismissing a worker. He does not know the correct procedure and may be accused of unfair dismissal. Full consultation should take place between the Marketing Department, Personnel Department and the legal adviser, before any decision is taken. The fact that this has not happened shows a lack of communication and suggests that this normally happens which is quite worrying. There is little point employing a legal adviser and then not making full use of her. Did he know about her presence? Did he know that he should confer with the Personnel Department?

The actions of one person may have serious repercussions for the firm in the future. If clear communication systems had been in place this would not have happened.

If a question refers to two cases and you only talk about one, then do not be surprised to score less than half marks, however good your answer is.

People in organisations

GRADE BOOSTER

Questions about 'people issues' at A2 level require a much more integrated approach.

People in organisations

Examiner's Commentary

(a) The first thing that Hugh should do is to gain more information about the accidents that have taken place, what department they occur in and how they happen. He should be looking for any patterns that may identify the reason for the accidents occurring. It may be that the accidents are mostly occurring in one department. It may also be the case that although accidents are occurring in different departments, their causes may be similar. Is it a lack of training, poor communication, poor management or a general lack of care amongst the workforce?

> A good start to the answer. A problem cannot be solved until the causes are known.

It is the managers of each department who are ultimately responsible for everything that happens within their department. Hugh will need to ensure that the managers are fully aware of the health and safety issues that are relevant. It is highly likely that there is much machinery and dangerous equipment involved in the production of office furniture. It may be that the obvious dangers are well protected. From the evidence about Bob, however, it may be that the more minor dangers are being ignored.

> This answer avoids the mistake of repeating legal facts. It is the application of law that is most important.

Once the causes of the accidents have been identified, Hugh will need to ensure that all managers and workers are clear about their own responsibilities. If necessary, better induction and training should be provided. There will be a cost involved; however, this cost must be weighed against the loss of earnings from regular accidents, never mind the potential bad publicity.

> This is the first step towards providing an evaluative answer.

The cause of the accidents may be less obvious. The time taken recently to gain ISO 9001 certification may have distracted everyone from other issues, and the fact that not everyone was happy with the changes may lead to a lack of motivation. Both of these factors may have meant that health and safety issues have been given a low priority recently. A look at the accident figures for the last few years will make interesting reading.

Once Hugh has identified all of these issues, he will have to establish an action plan or strategy to begin the task of minimising accidents in the future. Initially this may involve increased training and monitoring of workers. Those such as Bob may have to be formally reprimanded, which may eventually lead to dismissal, so that the message of safe working is taken seriously by all. A culture of safety in the workforce will require changes amongst managers and workers to reverse the recent trends.

> Good answers to this sort of question require a clearly thought-out strategy, as covered here.

(b) Circumstances surrounding both cases highlight serious communication problems at Bradley & Moores. The accident happened last week, but the Personnel Department have only just been made aware of it. Although you would not expect every single accident to be reported immediately to the Personnel Department, one as serious as this, where an employee will be missing from work, is something that will have an impact on the firm. Either the system of reporting accidents is inefficient so that the message does not get through quickly enough, or even worse, there is no clear system for communicating such matters. Information about accidents does not appear to be widely known. If Chelsea Rimmer, who is 'only' a legal adviser, is aware of the problem then so should the management in the company.

The lack of action by Bob's Line Manager shows poor communication, either because he did not know about the problem, or because he has failed to ensure that Bob did not improve.

The Marketing Manager has dismissed a member of staff without consulting the Personnel Department. This is very worrying as the Personnel Department is ultimately responsibly for the hiring and firing of all employees. The Marketing Manager may not have authority to dismiss workers, which may lead to claims of wrongful dismissal. He may be unaware of the legal issues involved, which may cost the company a lot of money in the future.

All of the above communication problems may be the result of the recent delayering exercise carried out by the firm. Although the eventual result of this process should be to improve the efficiency of communication, it may be that in the immediate term it has caused problems. This may be because managers and employees are not yet used to their new responsibilities or communication channels. Although we would expect things to improve with time this may not be before the problems created have had serious repercussions throughout the firm. For this reason it is imperative that the company approaches the correction of these communication problems with the highest priority.

The ability to suggest more than one cause will encourage analysis and evaluation in an answer.

A good holistic view of the problem that gains top marks.

People in organisations

Exam practice questions

BECKINGHAM FINANCIAL SERVICES LTD (BFS LTD)

Timothy Bright is one of five Regional Sales Managers for BFS Ltd. He was trying to prepare a presentation for the quarterly management team meeting to be held in four weeks. Kamal and Rashid Saddiqi, the joint Managing Directors of BFS, had recently decided that all the Regional Sales Managers should deliver a formal presentation which would give details of the performance of their region for the preceding quarter. Timothy had never done a presentation of this nature before, and was trying to anticipate what to include and what his audience might expect.

Timothy was concerned about the company's policy of paying all the Financial Advisers by commission on sales made. This method of remuneration does not provide them with any basic salary. This, he felt, was the main reason why he had problems maintaining levels of morale and motivation amongst his team of 20 Financial Advisers. Table 1 shows Timothy's own salary for the last five years, and his anticipated salary for the next year, 2003. As a Regional Sales Manager, he receives a modest fixed salary as well as commission on sales made by himself and his team.

Table 1

Timothy's Remuneration (commission) as a Financial Adviser (1998–2000)		
1998	1999	2000
£32 000	£36 000	£38 000

Timothy's Remuneration (including commission) since becoming Regional Sales Manager		
2001	2002	2003 (projected)
£28 800	£33 000	£39 000

The Saddiqi brothers had also instructed all the Regional Sales Managers to carry out monthly formal appraisals with members of their teams. This would include setting targets, monitoring performance and identifying training needs. Timothy was already expected to manage his own clients, meet monthly targets for the introduction of new clients, recruit new Financial Advisers and carry out all the responsibilities of a Personnel Manager, with only a secretary to help him. What he particularly lacked was any sophisticated knowledge of many of the relevant theories and concepts necessary to deal with these issues effectively. Timothy considered himself an effective salesman, as he had a sales record which was far superior to anyone else in the company. In the past he had suggested to the Saddiqi brothers that the company should centralise the personnel function and appoint an experienced Personnel Director. Timothy's view was that this would allow the Regional Sales Managers and their teams to concentrate on selling financial services.

The Saddiqi brothers thought that the additional expense of recruiting and paying a large salary to an experienced personnel professional would be a financial burden to their business. Timothy did not dare to question this as his predecessor had left rather suddenly after repeated arguments with the Saddiqi brothers concerning the severity of the monthly sales targets which they had imposed on the sales teams. Timothy decided that despite the extra workload and stress he felt it placed upon him, he would have to continue trying his best to cope.

People in organisations

1 **(a)** Calculate the percentage change in Timothy's salary between his **last year as a Financial Adviser** and:

    (i) his first year as a Regional Sales Manager [2]

    (ii) his projected earnings as Regional Sales Manager in 2003. [2]

(b) Discuss the appropriateness of the remuneration methods used by BFS. [15]

(c) Timothy believes that BFS should appoint a Personnel Director (line 34). Discuss the possible effects on BFS if such an appointment were made. [12]

2 Timothy has to prepare a presentation to the management team in four weeks time.

(a) Discuss how Timothy can ensure that his presentation is effective. [12]

The Saddiqi brothers have instructed the Regional Sales Managers to carry out monthly appraisals of their Financial Advisers.

(b) Discuss the implications for BFS of introducing an appraisal system. [15]

[OCR June 2003]

examiner's tip	These questions should be completed in 90 minutes.

People in organisations

Answers on pages 68–71 **Answers** on pages 68–71 **Answers** on pages 68–71

(1) (a) (i) Salary in 2000 – £38 000
Salary in 2001 – £28 800
Change in salary = £9 200 (1)

Percentage change $= \dfrac{£9\,200}{£38\,000} \times 100 = 24.2\%$ decrease (1)

(ii) Change in salary = £1 000 (1)

Percentage change $= \dfrac{£1\,000}{£38\,000} \times 100 = 2.6\%$ increase (1)

examiner's tip	Questions requiring percentage change calculations are common in Business Studies and are usually badly done by students.

(b) *Knowledge*

Remuneration methods include payment per hour, piece rate, commission based on a percentage of sales and salary. **(1–3 marks)**

Understanding/Application

- Those employees motivated by money will be happy with a performance related pay such as that operated by BFS Ltd as they will be encouraged to earn a lot of money.
- The lack of any non-commission component of salary may be seen as a demotivator, as an individual may be unable to earn a suitable minimum income to allow them to pay their regular bills. This lack of income may be partly out of the Financial Adviser's control. **(4–6 marks)**

Analysis

- The fact that the Financial Advisers only earn income if they sell may lead to ethical concerns about them trying hard to sell 'products' which make them the most commission, rather than ones that are the best for the client's particular needs.
- Commission only payment may be a factor contributing to the low levels of morale and motivation mentioned. It could be of considerable significance to the new recruits who may well struggle to make sales in the early stages of their new job. However, it could also give them the incentive to try hard from the beginning.
- It appears to be particularly unsuitable for encouraging the best Financial Advisers to become Regional Sales Managers. As can be seen from the earlier calculation Timothy saw a considerable decrease in his income in 2001 when he became a Regional Sales Manager. It has taken him another two years before he has regained a level of income he was earning when he was just a Financial Adviser. This may lead to the best Financial Advisers choosing not to take any promotion opportunities, so leading to less suitable and successful employees being promoted as they would not suffer the same fall in income. **(7–10 marks)**

Evaluation

- It may be more appropriate for BFS Ltd in the future to introduce some form of basic salary that would enable the Financial Advisers to have some security of earnings, so achieving the lower levels of Maslow's hierarchical needs. As a result they are less likely to be dissatisfied (a link with Hertzberg) and they may be less likely to leave.

- Introducing some form of minimum income that is not linked to sales may also affect BFS Ltd's ability to recruit sufficient and/or appropriate recruits. It may improve their reputation as an employer, particularly important in a strong labour market with little unemployment. **(11–15 marks)**

(c) *Knowledge*

A Personnel Director would have responsibility for issues related to workforce planning and control, such as recruitment, training, discipline and grievances.
(1–2 marks)

Understanding/Application

- The Regional Sales Managers will be able to spend more time on sales related issues and less time on personnel issues.
- A Personnel Manager may be better able to convince the Saddiqi brothers that paying by commission is having a negative impact on new employees.
- The Personnel Manager could take responsibility for introducing the proposed appraisal system. **(3–5 marks)**

Analysis

- Removing the personnel responsibilities from Timothy Bright may lead to be very motivating for him. He is spending far too much time on personnel matters at the moment and in the future would be able to concentrate more on the successful organisation and control of his region. On the other hand, some of the other Regional Managers who may enjoy the responsibility of looking after personnel issues may suffer from a fall in morale and motivation.
- The proposed introduction of a formal appraisal system will only add to the burden of the Regional Sales Managers. A Personnel Manager would have a much greater degree of knowledge, experience and expertise in designing and introducing an appraisal system.
- Having someone specifically responsible for personnel matters may lead to better and earlier monitoring of any employee related issues. This will lead to a happier and more efficient workforce that will also be more profitable for the company. **(6–8 marks)**

Evaluation

- The Saddiqi brothers do not appear to be in favour of a centralised approach to personnel, and even if they did change their mind and appoint a Personnel Director there is no guarantee that they would agree with anything he/she suggests. This could have a negative effect on the morale and motivation of the Personnel Director and limit any benefits to the workforce that could have occurred as a result of any changes.
- The view that a Personnel Manager would be a financial burden is a rather short-sighted one. The added cost of employing a Personnel Manager would probably be offset significantly in the long-run due to the reduced costs associated with a lower labour turnover and the higher sales levels of a more motivated workforce. **(9–12 marks)**

People in organisations

(2) (a) *Knowledge*

Use of diagrams, handouts, a PowerPoint presentation and clear structure to his talk will all lead to an effective presentation. **(1–2 marks)**

Understanding/Application

- Timothy could ask the advice of the other Regional Sales Managers.
- Practising the presentation in front of members of his department or a friend or family member will allow Timothy to 'fine tune' his presentation. The people listening to his presentation can offer advice on how to make it shorter or less boring. **(3–4 marks)**

Analysis

- Timothy has only four weeks to prepare the presentation and has never done one before. He needs to make the best use of the time available to plan and prepare effectively. He might feel the need to impress the Saddiqi brothers and the other managers. This will mean that he has to take it very seriously and prioritise the content, using a professional software package such as PowerPoint.
- Timothy must also consider the time factor. There will be four other presentations from the other Regional Sales Managers. If his presentation is too short he will not provide sufficient information and he may appear a less committed manager. However, if his presentation is too long the audience may be bored and his presentation will lose its impact. **(5–8 marks)**

Evaluation

- Timothy may decide to ask the Saddiqi brothers for more guidance on what the presentation should include. This will ensure that Timothy is able to meet his audience's expectations, so making it more effective.
- It is best that the method that Timothy uses is one that he is happy and confident with. For example, the use of PowerPoint may improve the quality of his presentation, but only if he knows how to use it. Poorly designed slides and mistakes in using the software will only lead to a less effective presentation than if Timothy had kept to a more traditional approach. **(9–12 marks)**

(b) *Knowledge*

Appraisal usually involves a face-to-face discussion in which one employee's work is reviewed by another, using an agreed and understood framework. **(1–3 marks)**

Understanding/Application

- Appraisal will allow the business to identify ways that performance of the Financial Advisers may be improved. It could also allow BFS Ltd to identify training needs and help the Regional Sales Managers to identify any problems they were not aware of.
- The Regional Sales Managers already have a lot of work to do and so may resent having to take on the task of appraising their teams.
- The Financial Advisers may feel that time spent taking part in the appraisal process is wasted as they could be spending that time selling and so increasing their commission earnings. **(4–6 marks)**

Analysis

- The Financial Advisers may welcome the opportunity to voice any concerns that they have. It may allow the perceived complaints about the commission-only payment system to be formalised. This may lead to the Saddiqi brothers becoming more aware that it is really a problem.

- However, someone will need to consider the system that could be adopted. This may be difficult with no Personnel Manager at the moment and therefore no knowledge within BFS Ltd of the right way of going about this.

- There may need to be some sort of trial run and both the Regional Sales Managers and Financial Advisers would probably need to receive training as to how the process might work. This would take time and prove to be expensive. **(7–10 marks)**

Evaluation

- The Saddiqi brothers have imposed this change without any consultation. This is likely to lead to greater resistance from both the Regional Sales Managers and the Financial Advisers.

- The potential benefits, mainly in the long-run would need to be weighed-up with the costs, mainly in the short-run. There is the effort and expense of setting up the system, as well as the initial reduction in efficiency that is to be expected when anything new is introduced. But there are potential benefits to be gained from the regular assessment of employees' performance, which may lead to greater motivation and efficiency gains for the whole organisation.

- What if the Regional Sales Managers and Financial Advisers were only to pay lip service to the process because it had been imposed on them? This will mean that the costs are felt by the business without any benefits in return. **(11–15 marks)**

examiner's tip	When asked about implications for a business of changing something, many candidates only talk about the advantages. The use of the word 'implications' is meant to imply that you should look at both the advantages and disadvantages. The best evaluative answers will try to weigh-up the overall impact on the firm.

Chapter 8

Operations management

Questions with model answers

C grade candidate – mark scored 10/20

Examiner's Commentary

Hollinshead Fabrics Ltd is a fast-expanding family firm that produces children's toys made from pieces of material that are stitched together by hand into animal shapes. The Operations Director, Imogen Hollinshead, has just learnt that an order placed by a large toy store has been returned because most of the stitching on the toys is fraying. She is concerned as this is the fourth order returned, from different retailers, this month. Imogen feels that it may be time to replace the traditional method of quality control at the end of the production line.

?
For help see Revise A2 Study Guide section 8.1

(a) Explain two possible costs of poor quality control for Hollinshead Fabrics Ltd. [6]

(b) Assess possible quality control methods that Imogen could put in place. [8]

(c) Analyse how Hollinshead Fabrics Ltd may gain from internal economies of scale. [6]

(a) Two possible costs are the materials that have to be scrapped and the costs of lost orders. Because products are faulty they will have to be thrown away and this will cost a lot of money. This means that the company will make less profit. Also, because of poor quality, the company will find it difficult to get more orders from this company and other toy shops. They will have to spend more money on advertising to regain the confidence of consumers.

If you do not make sure that your answer is specifically about the company you are given information about, it is very unlikely that you will get more than half marks for the question. Although there are some well-explained points, the answer lacks detail, and some of it is not related fully to the question asked.

(b) Imogen should increase the amount of quality control taking place. More people checking the work being done will help to identify the workers who are not good enough. These workers can then be replaced or retrained.

They may also want to increase the amount of machinery used. This will reduce the potential for human error, and so improve the reliability of output. Perhaps she should consider introducing the use of Computer Assisted Manufacturing (CAM), where the workers only have to push buttons on a machine to make sure that it does not go wrong.

This is a poor answer, because no attempt has been made to look at the implications of the suggestions made; for example, could a family firm afford to buy the CAM technology? There is also very little use of the case material.

(c) The company may gain purchasing economies of scale. This is because they may now be able to buy in bulk, which is usually cheaper per unit. They will also find it cheaper and easier to borrow money, as banks will be happier to lend money to larger firms, since they are less risky. Marketing economies may also be gained.

Although this student's answer shows evidence of knowledge, it does not contain any context. The key word in the question is analyse. This requires detailed discussion of links, implications and, if necessary, criticisms.

GRADE BOOSTER

If you compare this answer to the A grade answer you will see the main difference is the use of the information given about Hollinshead Fabrics in the question.

A grade candidate – mark scored 19/20

(a) One cost of poor quality control is the effect on the company's reputation. Any adverse publicity that may occur will be particularly bad for a small company such as Hollinshead Fabrics, as they will rely on 'word of mouth' to create orders from other firms. If a potential customer finds out about these returned products they may be reluctant to order from this company themselves.

> Recognition that being a small company will cause specific problems is good context.

A second cost will be that of reworking the returned products to bring them up to the standard required to make them saleable. Not only will the costs rise and hence profits be decreased, there is the potential knock-on effect of delays to other orders. Because the toys are handmade the workers will have to spend a great deal of time concentrating on the returned products, rather than producing new products.

> With 6 marks on offer for two costs, it is clear that the greater detail found in this answer is necessary.

(b) One possible system could be to introduce random checks, at all stages of the production line. However, the fact that the current system of quality control is not working may suggest that this system of a third party checking the work of others is not working. An alternative would be to introduce a system of Quality Assurance, maybe as part of a Total Quality Management strategy. It may be that the material is received from the supplier in a poor state. If quality control takes place at the end of the production line, this fault will not be noticed until a lot of work has taken place. Far better for this material to be identified as not being up to standard at an early stage.

If each worker is given responsibility for quality, this will not only increase the amount of quality checking taking place, but it will also make the workers feel more involved in the company, so increasing their motivation and sense of commitment to the company.

> As is expected in the A2 papers, this candidate has taken a strategic approach, examining the implications for the policies being suggested.

(c) Economies of scale arise when an increase in output leads to a fall in average costs. Internal economies are those that only benefit the individual firm.

> A clear definition of a difficult concept.

Hollinshead Fabrics may benefit from cheaper raw materials, because as they grow in size they will be able to buy in bulk, which usually reduces the unit cost. Financial economies may also be present. As the firm grows they will be able to negotiate cheaper rates when borrowing money and, because of their increased assets which act as security, they will be able to borrow more money.

However, they may find it difficult to benefit from technological economies of scale. As firms grow they are usually able to invest in more advanced and efficient technology. Given the highly labour-intensive nature of the fabric toys, it may not be possible to carry out the production by machine.

> Excellent use of context.

Operations management

WHITE MOUNTAIN GREETINGS PLC

White Mountain Greetings plc (WMG) manufactures and sells a wide range of consumable greetings products, including gift wrapping paper, accessories such as tags, ribbons and bows, together with Christmas and other cards and stationery. The business is one of the largest suppliers of own-label products to major UK supermarket chains, high street stores and specialist greeting card shops. Although the company manufactures a wide range of products, it generally targets the premium end of the market.   5

WMG has production facilities at a number of locations (see Fig. 1). The South Wales factory concentrates on accessories and crackers. Gift wrapping paper is manufactured in a new state-of-the-art plant in southern England, near Southampton. The stationery and greetings card plant is located near London.   10

Fig. 1

The London plant also has a warehouse where larger orders for all WMG's products are   15
brought together for packaging and dispatch. Nearby, on a high-tech business park, is
WMG's own research and design facility. This was established recently to create innovative
ranges of products as well as using licensed film, TV and computer-game characters and
images. Designs are targeted at various market segments such as children and students in
both the UK and USA.   20

Production planning is vital, especially for the Christmas market when 75% of sales occur.
Because of the seasonal nature of the products, WMG has to hold large volumes of finished
stocks, particularly during late summer and early autumn. This is a very busy time for the
Production Director, Amy Hunter, the Sales Director, Mike Fisher and the Senior Design
Manager, Suresh Amil. All production facilities operate five days a week, with any   25
maintenance carried out at weekends. From late summer however, all the company's plants
need to run at full capacity.

Planning has begun for a new range of products. The theme chosen is 'Conservation and
the Environment', an issue close to Amy's heart. She has concerns about the nature of the
company's products, which have a very short life and end up as waste soon after purchase.   30
She has been researching the sourcing of paper supplies from producers that can
manufacture the high quality paper needed for premium products, using eco-friendly
production processes. Although there are cost implications, she also wants to switch to
bio-degradable* printing inks.

biodegradable – capable of being decomposed by living organisms

Mike Fisher is excited about an enquiry he has just received from a French supermarket chain. It is interested in ordering some of WMG's designs of cards, stationery and gift wrapping paper under its own-brand range. This is WMG's first potentially large order from a major European retailer. However, Amy is not sure they can meet the delivery dates. Southampton operates a just-in-time stock holding policy and the high quality paper used has to be sourced from Belgium. Also, capacity at the London and Southampton plants will be taken up for the next nine weeks by orders from their existing customers. The French supermarket has specified that the order must be delivered to its central warehouse just outside Paris within the next twelve weeks. Amy has contacted the Production Managers at both factories with details of the French supermarket order, asking them for potential production planning schedules. She has then produced a table and network diagram so she can carry out a critical path analysis for the order. (See Table 1 and Fig. 2.)

Table 1 **WMG PLC – FORECAST ACTIVITY DURATION SCHEDULE**

French supermarket order

Activity	Task	Duration (days)
A	Final designs produced and sent for approval	3
B	Designs amended/accepted; order confirmed	2
LONDON Greetings card production:		
C	Preparation and setting of machines	2
D	Printing, cutting and finishing	4
E	Packing	2
SOUTHAMPTON Wrapping paper production:		
F	Materials ordered	1
G	Materials delivered	1
H	Preparation and setting of machines	1
I	Printing, cutting and finishing	3
J	Packing	1
LONDON Warehouse:		
K	Pallet order and load on containers	2
L	Delivery to Paris via Channel Tunnel	1

Operations management

Fig. 2

Network for French supermarket order

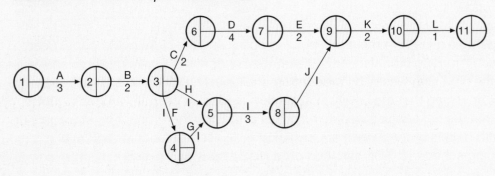

1 **(a)** 75% of WMG's sales are made to the Christmas market. Describe **two** operational problems this may cause the business. [4]

(b) The Board of Directors of WMG is considering centralising all production on one site. Evaluate the factors that might be considered by WMG when choosing a suitable location for the potential new plant. [12]

(c) Evaluate the benefits to WMG of having its own research and design facility (line 17). [12]

---

2 **(a)** Amy Hunter has produced a forecast activity duration schedule for the French supermarket order. Refer to Table 1 and Figure 2.

  (i) Calculate the earliest start time for the packing of the greetings cards and stationery at the London factory (activity E). [1]

  (ii) Calculate the latest finish time for the production of the wrapping paper at the Southampton factory (activity I). [1]

  (iii) Calculate the minimum time for the completion and delivery of the order to the French supermarket. [1]

  (iv) Freight train drivers at the Channel Tunnel have called a series of 48-hour strikes over the next 3 months. Briefly discuss the potential implications of this action for the order. [8]

  (v) Evaluate whether critical path analysis (CPA) is a useful technique for helping WMG plan its production. [9]

(b) Evaluate the implications for WMG of planning to manufacture an increasing proportion of its output using environmentally friendly resources. [10]

[OCR June 2003]

examiner's tip	These questions should be completed in 90 minutes.

Answers on pages 77–81 Answers on pages 77–81 Answers on pages 77–81

Answers

(1) (a) *Knowledge*

Possible operational problems include high storage costs, planning production schedules, flexibility of the workforce and quality issues. **(1–2 marks)**

Understanding/Application

- The need to concentrate the majority of production into a relatively short space of time will mean a larger number of part-time or temporary workers are required.
- At the very busy times of the year it will be difficult for WMG to take on special orders such as the French supermarket order. **(3–4 marks)**

examiner's tip 'Operational problems' must be to do with clearly production-based issues such as costs, capacity, productivity, stock, quality, production planning, production methods, location and labour flexibility. Problems related to marketing, personnel (motivation & recruitment) and finance would gain zero marks in this sort of question.

(b) *Knowledge*

Factors that need to be considered before selecting a suitable location include:

- Availability of labour skills
- Cost of the new site
- Possible grants available
- Proximity to suppliers and the market
- Availability of a suitable site. **(1–2 marks)**

Understanding/Application

- As WMG sell all over the UK the geographical location of any site is less important.
- The fact that the Southampton site is described as a 'new state-of-the-art plant' may mean that WMG are loath to move away from there. **(3–4 marks)**

Analysis

- If WMG see the French supermarket order as the beginning of an expansion into Europe then a location near to the Channel Tunnel in Folkestone, or a main airport such as Gatwick or Manchester may be more attractive.
- The nature of WMG's production using 'state-of-the-art' equipment will mean that the need for skilled labour is low. Given the highly competitive nature of the market that they are in it may therefore be best for WMG to target a location with plentiful unskilled and cheap labour.
- In addition, the fact that labour is relatively unskilled reduces the need to relocate the company's current employees if any move takes place.
- As WMG sells a lot of their output to 'major supermarket chains' a location close to customers is less of an issue. They would not be delivering directly to each supermarket. Supermarkets have a centralised distribution network and so it is likely that WMG would be expected to deliver their produce to a central or regional warehouse. This will reduce the amount of transportation needed to be carried out by WMG. **(5–8 marks)**

Evaluation

- Given the investment that WMG must have made in their Southampton site it may be the wisest option to create their one site there. This site is also nearby both ports, airports and is not too far from the Channel Tunnel. However, the London site is also close to their research & design facility, presumably with room for expansion on the high-tech business park.

- The employees that WMG will be least willing to lose in any relocation, and also the most expensive to make redundant and replace, will be the R&D staff and the managers (the latter presumably based in London as well). This may be a significant factor in making the final choice.

- Ultimately, WMG will also need to consider when to carry out the process of moving to the one site. It would be unwise to do this during the time of the year when WMG are in production for the busy Christmas market.

(9–12 marks)

(c) *Knowledge*

A Research & Design facility will allow a company to look at ways of improving the quality of a product and produce new product ideas. **(1–2 marks)**

Understanding/Application

- WMG would be able to look at ways of saving costs in the production of all their products, which would allow them to be more competitive.

- The Research & Design facility will be used to help Amy Hunter find products and production processes that are better for conservation and the environment. **(3–4 marks)**

Analysis

- WMG is aiming at the premium end of the market. With a Research & Design facility they can be seen as innovative, producing original and individual designs that are more likely to appeal to the premium end of the market. In other words, it will give WMG a useful USP.

- If WMG did not have its own Research & Design facility it would have to sub-contract out this procedure. This will be costly. Using a sub-contractor will also be time consuming, which may be important in the market that they operate in as it is very competitive and dynamic, with new designs and ideas always in demand.

- New and improved production methods could be researched to allow WMG to increase their productivity, which will help with the problems of most of their production being concentrated into a short period of time to satisfy the hugely seasonal market. **(5–8 marks)**

Evaluation

- Although there are many apparent benefits of WMG having their own Research & Design facility these will be felt over a long period of time. However, the initial costs of setting up and staffing the facility may have been better spent in other areas. Is the cost of sub-contracting out the Research & Design work offset by the benefits? Would the money needed for the in-house R&D facility have been better spent on improving quality or reducing production planning problems?

- In an industry such as 'consumable greetings products' is Research & Design such an important issue? It can be argued that in an industry such as the car industry new ideas and designs are vital for a competitive advantage. But is it really necessary for cards and wrapping products! **(9–12 marks)**

(2) (a) (i) Day 11 (1 mark)

(ii) Day 12 (1 mark)

(iii) 16 days (1 mark)

| examiner's tip | The completed earliest start times and latest finish times for Figure 2 are as follows: |

Node	Earliest Start Time	Latest Finish Time
1	0	0
2	3	3
3	5	5
4	6	8
5	7	9
6	7	7
7	11	11
8	10	12
9	13	13
10	15	15
11	16	16

(iv) *Knowledge*

The order may be delayed. An alternative form of transport may be used.

(1–2 marks)

Understanding/Application

- If WMG is unable to meet the delivery schedule for this order the French supermarket may not use them again.
- WMG may have to send the products by an alternative route, such as by air freight, which may be more expensive. (3–4 marks)

Analysis

- If the strikes happen during the time that WMG intend to deliver the finished products then they have a problem. Delivery is a critical task (Activity L) and there is only one day to complete it. The 48-hour strike will lead to a late delivery.
- WMG also rely on some raw materials being delivered from abroad. As WMG operate a JIT system and the high quality paper comes from Belgium, a 48-hour delay at this point will also have an effect. However, there are two days 'float' for Activity G and so it is possible that the strike will have no effect.
- The French order will take 16 days (just over 3 working weeks) but 9 out of the next 12 weeks are taken up by producing for existing customers. This implies that WMG will not have sufficient time to produce the French order, regardless of the possible strikes. (5–6 marks)

Evaluation

- Ultimately, it will depend whether WMG have any notice about when the strikes will happen. If they know sufficiently in advance then there will be less of a problem.
- WMG may delay a current order that is less important for one of their existing customers or may decide that in the interest of winning a potentially lucrative long-term order from abroad they get their employees to work some overtime to complete the order on time.

(7–8 marks)

(v) *Knowledge*

CPA can be used to aid planning and highlight potential problems.

(1–2 marks)

Understanding/Application

- Careful planning will show WMG the order in which events need to occur and the time taken. This will be useful for a company making so many different products for so many different customers.
- It will help WMG to make decisions about taking on extra orders such as the one from the French supermarket. **(3–4 marks)**

Analysis

- Resources can be ordered in advance. This is particularly vital for a company such as WMG that is using JIT. CPA allows the business to plan fairly accurately exactly when they will need to place an order for a particular component.
- CPA may highlight problems in meeting the order dates. This will allow WMG to be aware of the problem at the earliest opportunity to give them time to rectify it. **(5–6 marks)**

Evaluation

- Ultimately, CPA is only a diagram. Practical problems and/or poor management can still lead to orders not being completed on time.
- A company that is as complicated as WMG, with production and distribution on three separate sites, may find that CPA is unable to cope with so many variables. **(7–9 marks)**

(b) *Knowledge*

Increased output using environmentally friendly resources may lead to higher costs, marketing benefits and supply problems. **(1–2 marks)**

Understanding/Application

- The fact that there are generally fewer suppliers of environmentally friendly resources may have implications for stock levels at WMG.
- Environmentally friendly resources are usually more expensive, which may push up the price or reduce the profit margins of WMG. **(3–4 marks)**

Analysis

- For a company that is aiming its products at the premium end of the market, any increased costs leading to higher prices may be less of an issue. However, the supermarkets are normally very keen to force costs down and so WMG may have more difficulty in forcing through a price increase here.
- WMG are using JIT. This puts greater emphasis on reliability, in terms of timing and quality, of supplies. The fact that there may be fewer suppliers of the environmentally friendly resources may therefore cause problems for WMG.

(5–7 marks)

Evaluation

- The long-term savings may offset the increased costs and questionable availability of the environmentally friendly resources. Increasingly, businesses are being made responsible for the disposal of their products. It may also be possible that government taxes will be levied on firms that produce products that directly affect the environment's sustainability.

- The use of recycled paper, or paper made from trees harvested from sustainable forests is becoming much more of an issue for customers. However, most of the products currently available are not of a particularly high quality. If WMG could develop environmentally friendly products that were suitable for the premium end of the market then they would certainly have a competitive advantage. **(8–10 marks)**

examiner's tip

The range of questions asked on this particular paper is a good example of the different skills that examiners ask you to show. There are questions here about 'factors that might be considered', 'the benefits' and 'the implications' of a particular decision or course of action. It is vital that you are clear what **each** different question is asking you to do. To talk about factors when you have been asked about implications, or vice-versa, will lead to very disappointing results.

A2 Mock Exam 1

Business Studies

Time: 1 hour 30 minutes   Maximum marks: 120

Synoptic Paper 1   *BUSINESS STRATEGY*

Read the following extract then answer the questions which are based upon it.

Grading
Boundary for A grade   90/120
Boundary for C grade   60/120

CONTEXT
Hilldale Farm Ltd

Farming has been in crisis in the UK for at least a decade. Despite high food prices at the retail stage, prices received by farmers (so-called 'farmgate prices') have been falling, reaching their lowest level in real terms for 15 years in 2002. In addition, the high value of sterling compared with the currencies of rival food-producing countries had handicapped exports and also made it difficult to compete with imports. All these problems were compounded by the discovery of BSE or 'mad cow disease' in UK cattle in the 1990s. This long-lasting outbreak led to a ban on the import of UK meat products by many countries, including those of the European Union, causing exports to decline even further and leading to many farmers going out of business. Even for those UK food products which were not directly involved, there seemed to be a crisis of confidence abroad. Some details concerning recent trends in UK agriculture appear in **Appendix 1**.

Matters were then made even worse in 2001 by extremely wet winter weather which flooded much agricultural land. Then, most importantly, came the outbreak of foot and mouth disease in February 2001. A large number of countries immediately banned the import of meat from the UK. 2030 farms suffered an outbreak of the disease. In total, four million animals on 10 000 farms, mainly cattle and sheep, were destroyed. Markets and auctions were closed so that even healthy animals could not be sold or moved. Indeed, it was even impossible to move cattle and sheep from one field to another, and thousands had to be left in increasingly muddy and barren pastures. Thus, farmers whose animals did not catch the disease incurred great costs in feeding livestock which they would normally have sold. Veterinary costs also rose as animals could not be moved to more healthy conditions, notably in winter.

The closure of the countryside, for up to six months in some areas and nearly a year in the most affected regions, meant that the tourist trade in rural areas was seriously affected. Footpaths and bridleways were closed and farms and fields could not be entered. Hotels and Bed & Breakfast establishments also saw their trade collapse.

Hilldale Farm Ltd was one of the businesses affected by these disastrous events. The farm, owned and run by Tom and Christine Harrison, is situated at the end of picturesque Hilldale in the Peak District of

England. The road from the end of the Dale passes through the village of Hilldale before ending at the gates of Hilldale Farm. The farm experiences no through traffic and is somewhat isolated. However, the farm land is crossed by several footpaths and bridleways, and there is a steady stream of walkers and horse riders passing through in the tourist season.

Hilldale Farm Ltd has a flock of 600 sheep and a herd of 100 dairy cows. The business owns the farmhouse and its outbuildings. It also owns 180 hectares of land, 60 hectares being on the river valley floor, where the cattle graze, and 120 hectares in the surrounding hillside, where the sheep spend most of the year. Both the owners work on the farm, with part-time assistance from their two teenage children who are at school. Two full-time stockmen are employed. Some of the silage or animal feed is grown on the farm, but much has to be purchased. Sheep shearing and silage cutting are contracted out. Other expenditure includes vets' bills, fertiliser and pesticides, and diesel for the farm vehicles. Like all agricultural businesses, Hilldale Farm Ltd receives subsidies from the Government, the Agricultural Mortgage Corporation and the European Union, but it is not situated in a Less Favoured Area (as designated under EU legislation) and so does not receive the extra aid given to farmers in those regions.

Hilldale Farm Ltd did not suffer from foot and mouth disease, but it was subject to the restrictions on the sale and movement of animals, thus incurring extra costs of £10 000 for feeding stock in 2001. The business traded at a loss in that year and again in 2002, despite the fact that restrictions on sales were lifted. The prices of milk (18 pence per litre) and wool were low, lambs fetched as little as £20 each at the re-opened markets and the price of heifers varied between £500 and £800, a considerable reduction on the prices received before the restrictions were imposed. The extra costs incurred in keeping and feeding the animals during the period of the disease meant that the sale prices often did not cover costs. Tom Harrison sometimes thought that he would have been better off if his animals *had* caught the disease, as it was reckoned that there were as many as 47 farmers who had each received over £1 000 000 of compensation. Businesses like Hilldale Farm Ltd had received nothing of the £2.7 billion compensation paid out to farmers, whose stock had been slaughtered. In addition, the sheep subsidy was based on market prices, which were at rock bottom. Before the disease struck, Hilldale Farm Ltd had been trading at a profit, albeit a steadily declining one. In 2002 Christine Harrison had been forced to find some part-time work in the village teashop in order to supplement the family's income. The Profit and Loss Account for Hilldale Farm Ltd for 2002, with comparative figures for 2001, appears in **Appendix 2**.

It was clear to Tom and Christine Harrison that, if these trends continued, they would be forced, like four farms in neighbouring valleys, to go out of business. The Harrisons wished to stay in farming but realised that, like 65% of all farming businesses, they would have to diversify into other activities and thus adopt a new corporate strategy. Financially, the company is highly geared, 90% of the long-term finance coming from their bankers, who also supplied an overdraft facility. Some funding has also been received from government subsidies. Any diversification plan would therefore have to be approved by the bank, particularly if it involved further investment. The Curry Report (2002) was also a worry to all farmers including the owners of Hilldale Farm Ltd. This Report advocated the replacement or eventual abolition of traditional output-based subsidies with aid to those agricultural businesses that contributed to environmental and social development.

There was also the problem of public opinion. Although the area was traditionally reliant on agriculture and tourism, several people had recently moved into Hilldale and neighbouring areas who had no connections with these industries and at times even seemed to be hostile to developments that caused an increase in visitors and traffic. Several farmhouses in the area were occupied by people who commuted to work in the towns and cities of Yorkshire and Lancashire and had no connection with, or experience of, agriculture or rural life.

After considerable research and discussion the Harrisons came up with four alternative plans to discuss with the bank manager. All these were preliminary ideas. Any that warranted further research would need to be followed by a full business plan.

Plan A consisted of remaining in pastoral farming by merging with or taking-over other farms in neighbouring Dales and possibly specialising in rare breeds or expanding into beef cattle. Several farms had gone into liquidation, creating a pool of experienced labour. It might be possible to rent some of their land, now owned by non-farmers, for grazing and silage production.

Plan B involved expansion into the Bed & Breakfast business. The Harrisons had occasionally provided overnight accommodation to passing ramblers, but had not advertised or taken this option seriously. The Peak District and the Dales are relatively thinly populated but are very popular tourist areas for motorists and cyclists, with at least one former railway line converted to a cycle trail. The area is especially popular for both holiday walkers and serious hikers. The Pennine Way, a long-distance trail to the Scottish Borders, starts from Edale in the Peak District, and there are hundreds of other well signposted and mapped paths in the area. The industrial areas of Yorkshire and Lancashire, including the cities of Sheffield and Manchester, are within 20 or 30 miles and many people visit the Peak District at weekends from these large conurbations. The area had suffered from the closures in 2001 and some hotels and several Bed & Breakfast establishments had ceased to trade. However, tourism had recovered somewhat in 2002, reinforced by the reluctance of some people to holiday abroad because of fears of aircraft safety after the events of 11 September 2001.

Hilldale Farm Ltd had a derelict group of barns that could be converted into four accommodation units at an estimated cost of £100 000. Breakfast would be provided in the farmhouse and a price of £40 per room (£25 for single occupancy) would seem to be the going rate in the area. Planning permission would be needed, and local regulations stated that altered structures had to be in character with existing farm buildings (e.g. would have to be the same style of roof) and that agriculture must remain the main business of a farm which diversified.

Plan C involved creating a caravan site in one of the fields. This would involve conforming with the appropriate laws and regulations regarding, for example, water supply, drainage and sewage disposal, construction of hard standings and adequately surfaced areas. The Harrisons had occasionally allowed passing walkers to pitch their tents in their fields but had no experience of providing permanent sites. The proposed site would enable tourists to park their caravans overnight or for several days. Caravans would not be sited there for permanent use or for hire, although it might be possible to store caravans on the site in the winter for owners who did not want to use them all year round. Fees for all these services would have to be researched, as would the costs of setting-up the facility.

Plan D was to concentrate on providing leisure and educational pursuits. The river could be dammed to create and stock a fishing lake. Orienteering and guided walks were a possibility, as were areas for paintballing games. Guided educational visits for schools and other interested groups had been tried by some farmers and found to be popular. It might even be possible to convert the barns to either a suite of conference rooms or an educational centre, instead of overnight accommodation. Environmental grants were available to all farms which contributed to conservation and ecological schemes such as preservation of farm ponds and the erection or maintenance of hedges and drystone walls. Hilldale Farm Ltd had already received some income under these schemes and some of the ideas in Plan D might lead to an increase in the level of subsidies. Local councils might also contribute to schemes that provided for educational visits or conferences.

All four of these plans had serious implications in financial terms, particularly in the initial stages, but some would also involve extra labour costs and, in addition, might provoke environmental objections. It would also be necessary to forecast demand and a proper business plan would need to be constructed. Above all, the Harrisons were determined to stay in pastoral farming, regardless of any diversification that might occur. It was with some trepidation that they went to see the bank manager in May 2003.

APPENDIX 1

Recent trends in UK Agriculture

- The UK's dairy herd shrank by 14% and the beef herd by 7.2% between June 1995 and June 2000.

- Over 50 000 farmers and farm workers lost their livelihoods between June 1998 and June 2000.

- In 2001, the average profit earned by farmers was £5200 per annum.

- Hill farmers, rearing livestock, earned an average profit of £3500 per annum in 2001.

- Farmers often worked as much as 60 hours per week.

- The average age of a farmer had risen to 57.

- Investment was at its lowest level for 30 years in 2001, retained profits being insufficient to finance new investment.

- Short-term debts had risen and long-term liabilities were being called-in by lenders.

- The net worth of agricultural businesses had fallen by 20% in a five-year period.

Adapted from the following sources:
www.nfu.org.uk
Guardian Education, 5 February 2002: 'Crossroads in the Country'; John Crace.

APPENDIX 2

Hilldale Farm Ltd: Profit and Loss Account for years ending 31/12/2001 and 31/12/2002

	2001 £	2002 £
Sales Revenue (including subsidies)	130 250	161 750
Cost of Sales	150 750	142 180
Gross Profit	(20 500)	19 570
Operating Costs	9 400	8 600
Profit Before Interest and Tax	(29 900)	10 970
Interest	10 400	11 270
Tax	0	2 150
Retained Profit	(40 300)	(2 450)

NB no dividends were paid in 2001 or 2002.

1 Tom Harrison wishes, if possible, to remain in agricultural-based activities. Assess the extent to which Plans A and D may assist in this aim as well as ensuring the survival of the business. [40]

2 Christine Harrison thinks that Hilldale Farm Ltd's main problems are the seasonal variations in income and activities. With particular reference to Plans B and C, recommend a strategy which might succeed in coping with this problem. [40]

3 Assess ways in which Hilldale Farm Ltd could overcome any problems which diversification might create in the areas of human resource management and corporate culture. [40]

[Edexcel June 2003]

A2 Mock Exam 2

Centre number _____

Candidate number _____

Surname and initials _____

Business Studies

Time: 2 hours   Maximum marks: 80

Synoptic Paper 2   *BUSINESS STRATEGY*

Study the information and answer all parts of the questions that follows.

Grading
Boundary for A grade   56/80
Boundary for C grade   44/80

CUTTING AND TAYLOR (GARDEN CENTRE) LTD

Cutting and Taylor (Garden Centre) Ltd (C & T) is the legal identity of Lower Orton Garden Centre. Established in 1948 as a plant nursery it has since grown into a business with a turnover of about £2.2 m in 2002. Kevin Cutting, the founder's grandson, is Managing Director; his mother, Isabella, is Chair of the Board. Ownership of the company is held entirely within the Cutting family, the Taylors having been bought out in 1962.   5

The nature of the garden centre industry is seasonal. Traditionally, the spring bank holiday weekend is the busiest time of the year. Other periods of high demand are when bedding plants are being bought and in the run up to Christmas when gift sales are significant. Other than these specific peaks, demand tends to rise in the spring and summer and decline in autumn and winter. Although weather does tend to influence sales on a daily basis it is not a major factor over a period   10
of a few weeks. Customer numbers tend to be higher at weekends. During the week the typical customer is non-economically active, a gardening enthusiast who will visit C & T with a specific purchase in mind. This focus, however, does not stop them wandering throughout the garden centre looking at stock. In contrast, weekend customers are typically younger, less knowledgeable and far more willing to engage in impulse purchases. These customers are more readily influenced   15
by media and point-of-sale material than the experienced gardener. Their approach is increasingly to purchase large, mature plants that will not require years of nurturing to reach their full potential. Being mainly from socio-economic groups A, B and C1 Kevin describes them as 'cash rich, time poor'. Over the last three years Kevin has noticed a steady shift in C & T's customer base toward the inexperienced end of the scale. The variable pattern of sales, both weekly and annually, causes   20
a number of problems for C & T. These centre on cash flow, stock and employment levels.

Lower Orton Garden Centre employs 34 full-time equivalent staff. Of these 24 are full time, four being qualified horticulturalists with a National Diploma in Horticulture, NDH. A fifth full-time member of staff is currently working toward this qualification. At any one time at least one horticulturalist will be on duty and accessible to customers. Finding and retaining good staff is   25
an issue. The industry has a relatively unattractive image, with poor pay, long and unsociable hours, and unpleasant working conditions. It is Kevin's view that many of the qualities required

to be a good horticulturalist militate against being good at adopting a customer focus. It is only since becoming a manager that Kevin has fully understood one of his grandfather's favourite expressions: 'Plant people are not always people people'. Despite these issues C & T enjoys a good reputation for having knowledgeable staff. Staffing levels can be adjusted at busy times by using a greater proportion of part-time staff.

The company owns the site from which it operates. The company's bankers have made it clear that they would be willing to advance capital given this potential security. The site is split into four main sections. The largest is the area dedicated to rearing plants, such as pansies and geraniums. C & T buy in its stock of shrubs, trees and exotic plants. The second section is the selling area. This comprises six large sheds and an outdoor display area. (One shed houses garden tools and equipment, and another gifts, while the remaining four are used to display plants.) The third section is a restaurant, while the fourth section is the car park.

The restaurant was opened six years ago. Operated as an autonomous profit centre, it is now regarded as an essential part of the C & T product portfolio, see Table 1. Each quarter Kevin holds a meeting to discuss financial targets and so allocate resources. From these meetings Kevin is increasingly aware that some restaurant customers do not buy anything other than their refreshments when they visit C & T. Consequently, whilst customer numbers might rise at busy periods some do not arrive with the intention of buying plants. Although he has no hard evidence, he suspects that for some customers C & T is an entertainment destination rather than a garden centre. This view is supported by some non-restaurant staff, some of whom feel that the presence of these customers devalues the integrity of the garden centre as a serious horticultural proposition. Kevin is rather unsure whether this is an issue. On the one hand he is glad that the restaurant yields income. However, on the other he feels the traffic generated by restaurant visits should be leading to more sales income, especially of non-restaurant purchases. He thinks it should be easier to gain sales from existing customers than to gain sales by attracting more customers. Such an approach would lessen the car park capacity problems that C & T experiences at weekends. At the moment C & T does not advertise because an analysis three years ago suggested it was not cost effective.

Table 1. Profit centre performance £'000s

	Plants	Gifts	Equipment	Restaurant	Total
Sales	744	516	388	558	2206
Gross profit	371	310	261	419	1361
Net profit	104	43	(7)	152	292

As Managing Director, Kevin's attention is frequently focused on the long-term success of the business. He believes his role is to support his staff in the day-to-day operations, allowing them to decide on stock levels, display and staff rotas. His role is to explore how C & T can continue to grow as a business so as to provide an acceptable income for its various stakeholders. Historically, sales have grown steadily, with a noticeable upturn in growth in the last five years. Kevin attributes this to increased media exposure of gardening and garden design. Profits have also grown, but at a slower rate over this same period. Arresting the decline in the profitability of the business is one of Kevin's key concerns.

The rise in the popularity of garden design has caused Kevin to consider diversifying such that C & T can offer customers a complete range of products for the garden. For example, at the moment C & T only sells small bags of gravel, a few timber stakes and other materials such as timber preservatives. Customer enquiries about decking and sheds, for example, have to be turned away. Through his business contacts Kevin is aware that the town's builders' merchant is about to come onto the market because the owner is retiring. The general view amongst Kevin's business contacts is that the owner has lost interest. Consequently, it is now not particularly successful. The commercial estate agent has provided Kevin with some brief background notes about the builders' merchant (see Appendix 1). Kevin believes the synergistic benefits of such a purchase are clear.

The garden centre industry is becoming increasingly concentrated. Small independent operators are being squeezed by a combination of multiple centres, such as Wyevale, and out of town DIY superstores, such as B & Q. Kevin believes C & T has clear competitive advantages with regard to choice and quality. However, he is less confident about the business' ability to match the larger companies when it comes to marketing. Joining a regional group of independent centres has, to a limited extent, offset some of the cost disadvantages of being considerably smaller. There are nonetheless other areas in which C & T could not expect to be competitive. This is one reason that the diversification offered by buying a builders' merchant seems attractive.

Kevin is considering two other options for C & T to pursue, both of which have a common root in landscaping. The first is to contract with house builders to undertake the initial garden design and landscaping for their new developments. Each contract would be for a fixed price and would cover such issues as design, layout and the landscaping of individual gardens. The other option is to build upon C & T's good reputation and offer a garden design and maintenance service in the locality. To begin with, Kevin has attempted a SWOT analysis, see Figure 1. Kevin can foresee few problems in competing successfully with established firms, given C & T's strengths.

Figure 1

SWOT analysis of C & T
(Garden design and maintenance)

Strengths	Weaknesses
C & T's local reputation as a garden centre Horticultural expertise Could source plants at low cost	Scarcity of resources: capital and manpower Divert management attention Unable to protect design ideas
Opportunities	**Threats**
Competition fragmented; several sole traders Low barriers to entry/exit and sunk costs Market growing in size	Established competition Market income sensitive

The direction in which he should take C & T is a decision that will need very careful thought. Although organic growth continues to be an option, Kevin feels that if the company is to be successful, C & T should seek external growth. With the exception of an intermittent overdraft, C & T has no debt and could readily borrow, using the site as collateral, if necessary (see Appendix 2). He is mindful that as Managing Director he is custodian of the business and he cannot afford to make an incorrect choice.

APPENDIX 1

Outline details (without prejudice) of

Business:	Miner's Building Supplies Ltd
Location:	Station Road, Upper Orton
Site value:	£350 000 (with current planning permissions; commercial)
2002 Turnover:	£218 000
Staff:	12

Offers in the region of £850 000
To be sold as a going concern

APPENDIX 2

Cutting and Taylor (Garden Centre) Ltd
Balance Sheets as at end of financial year

		2002 £000s	2001 £000s
Fixed assets			
Tangible assets		565	523
Current assets			
	Stock	234	190
	Debtors	63	33
	Cash	598	584
		895	807
Current liabilities			
	Creditors	290	335
Net Current assets		605	472
Net assets employed		1170	995
Share capital		200	200
Profit and loss account		970	795
Capital employed		1170	995

1 Evaluate whether or not C & T should buy the builders' merchant. [18]

2 Discuss how C & T might secure the resources required, should it diversify into landscaping. [19]

3 Evaluate how Kevin might assess the effectiveness of the garden centre. [19]

4 Discuss the possible actions that C & T may have to take in the light of its changing customer base. [20]

[OCR June 2003]

A total of four marks are awarded for quality of written communication.

A2 Mock Exam Answers

SYNOPTIC PAPER 1

Question 1

Relevant points concerning the extent to which **Plan A** may assist Tom to stay in agricultural-based activities, and also ensure the survival of the business, include:

- If there is to be an expansion of farming, the farm may benefit from economies of scale, reducing unit costs and making it more competitive. However, there will be an increase in some of the farm's variable costs such as cattle feed, which will need financing.
- There is evidence in the case study – the mention of former farmers and farm staff – that the area is likely to have plenty of skilled labour from which to recruit.
- The Harrisons have expertise in pastoral farming that could be used to good effect. They may also find there is a niche market for the special breed of cattle: however, they may need to develop further expertise in this area, and may also need to research further into the demand for the special breeds.
- There remains the possibility of further outbreaks of disease, or other negative effects (e.g. climate change) on agriculture, and the Harrisons are concentrating on a relatively limited 'product'.
- The Harrisons are likely to be able to use the farm as collateral when obtaining finance, but there remain the costs of purchase.

Relevant points concerning the extent to which **Plan D** may assist Tom to stay in agricultural-based activities, and also ensure the survival of the business, include:

- Regarding the proposals concerning education and environmental conservation, unlike Plan A there is no evidence that the Harrisons have expertise in these areas.
- There will be a need to research into pricing and other marketing issues, and likely overall demand, since the case study indicates that the local area is not heavily populated.
- Some in the local area may object to certain activities such as paintballing, although the 'environmentally friendly' aspect of this Plan should lead to positive publicity for the farm.
- Plan D may well be the least costly plan, although there will be additional costs such as tour guides to conduct visits, or the Harrisons may have to commit their own time.
- However, Plan D may also generate the lowest revenue although this is likely to be spread reasonably evenly throughout the year.
- It is likely that the Harrisons could obtain grants from the government and/or the local council, although additional finance would still probably be needed.

In conclusion, there is no one guaranteed solution to the Harrisons' problems, and the possible returns from either or both plans may not guarantee survival. The Harrisons may prefer to diversify, even given its attendant risks, or they may choose to continue surviving by concentrating on farming, even given a relatively small profit.

1–8 marks   – *Knowledge of relevant areas, or simple descriptive comments about the case study information.*

9–16 marks   – *Application of theoretical points to Hilldale Farm's situation, and to the Plan(s) in the question.*

17–28 marks – *Analysis of Hilldale Farm's situation, and how this affects the likelihood of success with Plan A and/or Plan D.*

29–40 marks – *Evaluation of Plan A and Plan D, by presenting balanced arguments for and against both plans, using relevant information drawn from the case study.*

Question 2

Relevant points concerning a strategy for coping with the problem of seasonality, with particular reference to **Plan B**, include:

- With reference to the 'B&B' proposal, the Harrisons will have to research into the local market and demand, to see if it has reached saturation, and to check competitors' prices.
- There may be objections from local people, for example from existing competitors in the 'B&B' market, or from locals if traffic is likely to increase in the area as a result of implementing this plan.
- The nature of the tourist trade also needs researching: for example, how permanent is it likely to be?
- The location of the farm is not promising for tourism, since it is in an isolated position, and any further countryside closures would badly affect this proposed plan.
- Trade is also likely to be seasonal unless something can be done to boost trade in the winter season.
- Research is needed into whether permission to convert the buildings will be granted, as well as how the £100 000 is to be raised (will the bank lend it, even given the collateral available?) and at what cost.
- Costs may need further review: the Harrisons must accept that additional variable costs (e.g. extra labour, laundry and food costs) will be incurred, marketing-related costs will also arise (e.g. advertising the new service), and Christine may have to forsake her part-time job.
- There is no evidence that the Harrisons have appropriate expertise in this area, and therefore they may need to recruit additional staff since they are not likely to be able to find time to train themselves.

Relevant points concerning a strategy for coping with the problem of seasonality, with particular reference to **Plan C**, include:

- Costs remain a concern: for example, there are likely to be high start-up costs, and conversion and legal costs must also be met.
- However, variable costs are likely to be low, for example because there seems no need to employ additional staff unless extra security is required, although there are likely to be marketing-related costs due to the farm's location.
- There is no indication whether any finance is available to help meet any of the likely additional costs.
- Market research into the likely demand, the proposed pricing policy, and the nature of any local competition, is needed. There will, for example, be little in the way of 'passing trade'.
- The relationship with the farm may need further consideration: for example, would there be any likely negative effects on existing farming activities (e.g. any effect on livestock)?
- There may be complaints or objections from local people, for example on environmental grounds.

In conclusion, the Harrisons have recognised there is a seasonality problem and have produced two plans, either of which may partially overcome it. With both plans there remains a need for further market research, and to establish more clearly relevant costs and the availability of finance. Plan B may be the better plan for overcoming seasonality problems, since a more suitable marketing strategy (e.g. advertising and setting lower prices for the off-season) and financial strategy (e.g. arranging overdraft facilities in the off-season) can be set to help cope with seasonality.

1–8 marks – *Knowledge of seasonality, or simple descriptive comments drawn from the case study information.*

9–16 marks – *Application of the problem of seasonality to Hilldale Farm's situation, and a suggestion of simple ideas to help overcome it.*

17–28 marks – *Analysis of Hilldale Farm's situation, and how this affects the likelihood of overcoming seasonality with Plan B and/or Plan C, but without producing a convincing strategy.*

29–40 marks – *Evaluation of Plan B and Plan C, by presenting balanced arguments for and against both plans relating to seasonality, and an appropriate strategy to overcome the problem.*

Question 3

Relevant points concerning ways in which Hilldale Farm Ltd could overcome problems that diversification might create in the area of **HRM** include:

- The plans – especially Plan A – suggest that additional labour is likely to be needed. The staff may be part-time or temporary, or (in the case of Plan A) permanent.
- There is no evidence in the case study that the Harrisons are skilled in the HRM area. As a result, they may experience problems when recruiting and supervising the new staff.
- The Harrisons will also have to demonstrate suitable leadership, interpersonal and organisational skills to prevent staff from becoming overloaded with work at peak (e.g. seasonal) times.
- If some staff are laid off, e.g. as a result of any merger that takes place, there will be problems of morale and motivation for the remaining staff, with which the Harrisons will need to deal.
- They will also need to develop skills in dealing with those from outside the world of farming, e.g. visiting groups, tourists.

Relevant points concerning ways in which Hilldale Farm Ltd could overcome problems that diversification might create in the area of **corporate culture** include:

- The creation of a new workforce, and new business aims/objectives, should lead to a new corporate culture being developed.
- The core business of Hilldale Farm Ltd is likely to remain agriculture, although other priorities and goals may emerge that will affect the farm's corporate culture.
- There are likely to be a number of culture clashes. These could arise, for example as a result of any merger taking place, and also through employing new staff who may not share the existing or emerging culture of the farm.

In conclusion, much will depend on the Harrisons in terms of their commitment, attitude, leadership and organisational skills. They appear to be limited by an apparent lack of experience outside the world of farming. In order to overcome the potential problems outlined above, there may be a need for the Harrisons to receive training in the skills of managing and supervising staff. They will also need to be able to deal efficiently and effectively with visitors and the new staff, and to establish appropriate communication procedures with these people.

1–8 marks – *Knowledge of HRM and/or corporate culture, or simple descriptive comments drawn from the case study.*

9–16 marks – *Application of HRM and/or corporate culture theory to the Harrisons' situation, presenting some simple ideas in context.*

17–28 marks – *Analysis of the problem that diversification will cause, with some ideas for its solution, but without producing a balanced argument.*

29–40 marks – *Evaluation of the problem, by presenting balanced arguments relating to HRM and corporate culture, together with an effective assessment of how to overcome the problem.*

A2 Mock Exam Answers

SYNOPTIC PAPER 2

(1) Issues that are relevant and may need to be considered in making a decision to buy the builders' merchant include:

- The asking price of £850 000 is 3.9 times turnover and 2.43 times site value. If profit margins were even 10% then the payback period is 39 years! However, we are told that the owner has lost interest and so the recent turnover figures may be unduly low and Kevin may be able to buy the business for a lower price.
- For Kevin it is uncertain whether the builders' merchant represents new customers or existing customers. There is unlikely to be much overlap concerning the products sold, although they do complement each other to a large degree. We are told about the increased popularity in garden maintenance and C & T are currently turning some customers away.
- This means that if using Ansoff, the decision is one of product development (new product, existing customers) or diversification (new product and customers). Knowing this Kevin can assess the risk involved and therefore the price he is willing to pay.
- What are the benefits that C & T might gain? Risk may be spread, although both markets might be regarded as sensitive to the economic cycle. Might the garden design market be a passing 'fashion'? Buying the builders' merchant might help C & T's entry into the landscaping sector. It may also be less seasonal. Will the new purchase divert too much cash and attention away from the core business of C & T?

1–3 marks – Unsupported comments about buying the builders' merchant.

4–7 marks – Understanding shown about the reasons to be considered.

8–12 marks – Analysis to support any views given.

13–18 marks – A balanced argument is made, with a clear decision supported.

(2) A number of resources will need to be secured:

- Assuming that C & T does not have the cash then it needs to acquire additional funds, either debt or equity. This decision will be affected by the impact on gearing, the forecast for interest rates and the views of shareholders. If C & T will accept 25% gearing then it can borrow £390 000. There might also be scope for squeezing resources from current assets (Current Ratio = 3.1 and Acid Test Ratio = 2.3). In fact, restoring the Current Ratio to 2001's value would release £196 000.
- Where from and how will staff be recruited? Landscaping is fundamentally the same business as C & T are currently in, although the quantity of staff needed will depend upon which market is served. Can they use C & T staff in quiet periods? Might C & T's horticulturists already have the expertise needed for the designing?
- C & T will be able to provide the plants etc. for landscaping at cost price and so increase the profit potential.

Before any decision can be made C & T needs to establish what it is trying to achieve in strategic terms. Landscaping for new homes will present least problems as expansion capital can be generated by the business itself and staffing will be more easily managed with current resources or by using part-time or temporary staff.

A key consideration is how big will landscaping be? The larger it is the more formalised the resourcing required. Also, a manager may be needed, otherwise Kevin may take his eye off the main business.

1–4 marks – Possible sources of resources identified.

5–8 marks – Possible sources are described in the context of C & T.

9–13 marks – Resources discussed supported by analysis of the case material.

14–19 marks – Evaluation of resources required with some consideration of the company's objectives and strategic planning.

(3) Effectiveness assumes that some objective against which to measure current performance is identified.

- Table 1 shows that the company as a whole is clearly profitable. However, some profit centres are doing better than others. Gifts and Equipment are doing less well than Plants and Restaurant. However, all profit centres make a contribution and are mutually complementary so closing one down might reduce the sales made by another. Net profit margin compared to gross profit margin is particularly poor for Gifts and Equipment. However, this may be due to poor allocation of indirect costs and overheads giving an unfair reflection of these profit centres' performance.

- ROCE = 25%. However, some basis for comparison is needed to make this figure meaningful. Could Kevin gain such information from other businesses in the regional group of independent garden centres he has joined?

- Effectiveness may be assessed against a budget. Kevin could set budgets for each aspect of the business that could then be used to judge how each profit centre has done. But each profit centre does not operate independently. Poor weather will reduce customers visiting the garden centre, which will also affect sales in the restaurant.

- Measuring effectiveness of employees is more difficult. It could be achieved using a combination of sales, customer comments and absenteeism. The problem lies in assessing individual employees in an essentially service-sector situation. Many employees are not in a position to directly affect their performance, e.g. those working on the tills may not be able to boost sales; how much they take is determined by the time of week.

1–4 marks   – Knowledge of possible methods stated.

5–8 marks   – Description of methods that could be used in context.

9–13 marks – Case material is analysed to discuss the effectiveness of different methods.

14–19 marks – A balanced discussion that evaluates the effectiveness of different methods.

(4) Changing the customer base means changing the internal behaviour of the business for all functions. However, too much change runs the risk of alienating the core of serious gardeners that make purchases all the year.

- Marketing
  - New customers will be more receptive to advertising so C & T might need to reassess its view on advertising, especially as we are told that the analysis is dated.
  - Increased emphasis on point of sale material and visual appeal of merchandise become more important because of the impulse nature of the new customers. But C & T needs to be careful not to alienate its traditional gardeners.
  - The product mix will need to be changed with less need for small plants – although will this have an impact on cash flow?
  - If new customers are less price sensitive then prices can be raised.

- Operations
  - Stock control is less important as the type of plants being bought are less time critical. Less knowledgeable customers might be less aware of quality – although this could affect repeat purchases.
  - A switch to buying in plants would mean freeing up the rearing area for additional sales space.

- Finance
  - Sales should increase, as customers are 'cash rich'. This will impact on cash flow.
  - More new gardeners are likely to buy tools and equipment. This will help to increase profits in this profit centre as there should be no increase in overheads.
  - In addition, the new customers are more likely to have children with them and so gift sales should increase. If more families see a visit to the garden centre as a 'trip out' then more sales will be made in the restaurant for lunches and afternoon tea.
- Human Resources
  - Changes in customers means more emphasis on sales at weekends and holidays. This will impact upon staff rotas and numbers during the week. It might mean a reduction in full-time staff and more weekend/part-time staff. This may also impact on morale as working patterns and practices change.
  - Staff now need to be more knowledgeable as customers know less themselves. This has a training implication. More staff may also be needed in the restaurant.

1–3 marks – *Changes suggested not in the context of the case study.*

4–8 marks – *Changes are suggested that apply to C & T.*

9–14 marks – *Analysis of case material supports any changes suggested.*

15–20 marks – *An overall view is reached having evaluated different possible changes.*